Sunset

Low Cholesterol
COOK BOOK

By the Editors of Sunset Books and Sunset Magazine

in collaboration with
Patricia Kearney, R.D.,
Clinical Dietitian, Stanford University Hospital,
Stanford, California

Heart-healthy Chicken Yakitori (recipe on page 12)

Lane Publishing Co. ■ Menlo Park, California

Take Heart!

Research & Text
Sue Brownlee

Coordinating Editor
Deborah Thomas Kramer

Design
Joe di Chiarro

Illustrations
Dick Cole

Photography
Kevin Sanchez

Food & Photo Stylist
Susan Massey-Weil

Health-conscious individuals today make it a priority to eat foods that are low both in cholesterol and in fat. But it can be a challenge to prepare such healthful meals at home without compromising on portion size or flavor.

To help you meet this challenge, here's a marvelous collection of recipes that both conform with the American Heart Association's (AHA) requirements for fat intake and have no more than 100 milligrams of cholesterol per serving. Based on fresh ingredients that are easily available, our recipes are not only good for you but good-tasting, too.

From appetizers to desserts and from treats for kids to breakfast ideas, we offer a full range of dishes for every occasion. An appendix in the back of the book includes a glossary of terms, the AHA diet, and nutritional information for frequently used foods.

For our recipes, we provide a nutritional analysis (see page 6) prepared by Hill Nutrition Associates, Inc., of New York. We are grateful to Lynne Hill, R.D., for her advice and expertise.

We thank Rebecca LaBrum for her skillful and careful editing of the manuscript. We also thank Laurin Guthrie and Christopher Coughlin for their help with photography; Vignette, Sue Fisher King, Fillamento, Cookin', and Cottonwood for props used in our photographs; and Schaub's Meat Fish & Poultry, Monterey Market, and Cal Mart Grocery for their generosity and help.

Cover: Fresh Vegetables with Fettuccine (recipe on page 49), Golden Pepper Salad (recipe on page 73), Chewy Bread Sticks (recipe on page 86), and Creamy Chocolate Roll (recipe on page 89) are low in cholesterol, low in fat, but high in taste appeal. Design by Susan Bryant. Photography by Kevin Sanchez. Food and photo styling by Susan Massey-Weil.

About the Recipes

All of the recipes in this book were tested and developed in the *Sunset* test kitchens.

Food and Entertaining Editor, Sunset *Magazine*
Jerry Anne Di Vecchio

Editor, Sunset Books: Elizabeth L. Hogan

First printing January 1990

Contents

Special Features

Heart-healthy Eating

Take heart in the good news! You can reduce your risk of heart disease by reducing your blood cholesterol level. From chili to chocolate cake, pizza to peach cobbler, our recipes and tips will help you set up a low-cholesterol, low-fat eating plan you'll be happy to follow. Your diet makes a difference: eating right today can mean a healthier heart tomorrow.

Before beginning a low-cholesterol diet, you'll need to know a few facts. Here and on page 6, you'll find answers to some common questions about fat and cholesterol.

▪ What is cholesterol?

Cholesterol is a waxy, odorless, fatlike substance, used in the body for the synthesis of vitamins and hormones, the formation of nerve sheaths and cell membranes, and a number of other purposes. Cholesterol is found in all foods of animal origin.

There are two kinds of cholesterol. Some cholesterol, enough for the body's needs, is manufactured in the liver; *dietary cholesterol* comes from the food you eat. Both types affect the amount of cholesterol circulating in the bloodstream. Your *blood cholesterol level* is measured in milligrams (mg) per deciliter (dl).

▪ Why is your blood cholesterol level important?

The higher your blood cholesterol level, the greater your chances of developing heart disease. When too much cholesterol is carried in the blood, it builds up on artery walls and eventually narrows the artery—a process known as *atherosclerosis.* Atherosclerosis may ultimately result in a heart attack, since arteries can become so clogged that blood flow to the heart is blocked. (Other factors also increase the risk of heart attack, among them high blood pressure, cigarette smoking, obesity, diabetes, vascular disease, a family history of heart disease, and simply being male.)

Like other fatty substances, cholesterol doesn't mix with water; it's carried through the blood in protein "packages" called lipoproteins. *Low-density lipoproteins* (LDLs) carry the cholesterol that builds up in arteries and thus are often labeled "bad cholesterol." *High-density lipoproteins* (HDLs), frequently called "good cholesterol," help remove cholesterol from the artery walls, carrying it back to the liver for elimination.

In general, the lower the total level of blood cholesterol and LDL (and the higher the HDL level), the better. The National Cholesterol Education Program, organized by the National Institutes of Health and other health organizations, has issued the following guidelines for adults 20 years of age or older.

	Total Blood Cholesterol	LDL-Cholesterol
Desirable	Less than 200 mg/dl	Less than 130 mg/dl
Borderline-high	200–239 mg/dl	130–159 mg/dl
High	240 mg/dl and above	160 mg/dl and above

An HDL reading below 35 mg/dl is also considered a risk factor.

Reducing total blood cholesterol (and LDLs in particular) decreases the risk of heart disease, not only by slowing cholesterol buildup in arteries, but also (in some cases) by actually reversing the process.

▪ How do you lower your blood cholesterol level?

It's a two-pronged attack. First, reduce your intake of dietary cholesterol; the American Heart Association recommends less than 300 milligrams per day. This means limiting your consumption of animal foods such as meat, poultry, fish, eggs, and dairy products; organ meats and egg yolks are particularly high in cholesterol. Foods of plant origin, such as fruits, vegetables, grains, and vegetable oils, contain no cholesterol.

A second crucial step in lowering blood cholesterol, even more important than cutting dietary cholesterol, is restricting your intake of fat—in particular, saturated fat.

▪ What is saturated fat?

The fats we eat are made up of *saturated* and *unsaturated* fatty acids; unsaturated fatty acids are further classed as *polyunsaturated* or *monounsaturated.* Though food fats contain a mixture of all types of fatty acids, they're labeled saturated, polyunsaturated, or monounsaturated according to the kind present in largest proportion.

Saturated fat is the greatest dietary contributor to increased blood cholesterol. Often solid at room temperature, it's usually found in foods of animal origin: whole milk, cream, whole-milk dairy products such as cheese, butter, and ice cream, and red meats (the fat surrounding and running through meats is saturated). Poultry, fish, and shellfish contain saturated fat in lesser amounts. It's also found in some plant products—vegetable fats such as coconut oil, palm kernel oil, palm oil, and cocoa butter, for example. *Hydrogenated* vegetable oils (those that have been converted to solid or semisolid form by the addition of hydrogen) are higher in saturated fat than the unhydrogenated forms. Margarine and shortening are examples of hydrogenated fats.

Unlike saturated fat, polyunsaturated and monounsaturated fats can help lower blood cholesterol. Olive and canola (rapeseed) oils are sources of monounsaturated fat; safflower and corn oils are sources of polyunsaturated fat.

What is the ideal fat intake?

The American Heart Association and National Research Council recommend a daily fat intake of 30% or less of total calories, with less than 10% from saturated fat. In this book, we've calculated the percentages of fat for you—the fat calories in each recipe make up 30% or less of the total. Of course, all our recipes are low in cholesterol, providing 100 milligrams or less per serving. You can mix and match the choices here to create a wide variety of appealing and delicious menus; just keep in mind that your total daily cholesterol intake should be under 300 milligrams.

What are other steps to lowering blood cholesterol?

Besides eating less cholesterol, total fat, and saturated fat, you should lose weight if you need to; overweight individuals often have high cholesterol levels. By shedding excess pounds, exercising, and quitting smoking (if you're a smoker), you can both bring down your total blood cholesterol and help raise your level of HDL ("good cholesterol").

If you stick to a lowfat diet, you may find that you lose weight almost automatically. Fat is high in calories, supplying 9 calories per gram as compared to only 4 per gram for protein and carbohydrates (starches and fiber). According to the American Heart Association, about 55% of your total caloric intake should come from carbohydrates. To achieve that goal, eat plenty of vegetables, fruits, grains, legumes, and eggless pasta—foods containing complex carbohydrates, little or no saturated fat, and no cholesterol.

Moderate amounts of protein—about 15% of the day's total calories—are appropriate to a healthful diet. The American Heart Association recommends no more than 6 ounces of meat, fish, or poultry (cooked) per day, no more than 4 eggs per week.

How do you switch to low-cholesterol cooking?

Our recipes make it easy to enjoy a heart-healthy diet. This book will help you plan appetizing meals rich in vegetables, fruits, grains, and legumes; many poultry, meat, and fish dishes are also included. We use a variety of ingredients naturally low in fat and enhance their flavors with herbs and spices.

Cooking methods are lowfat, too—baking, barbecuing, poaching, steaming, and frying with the bare minimum of oil. Because a microwave can cook food in its own moisture without added fat, using this cooking method can also help to lower the fat content of your favorite dishes.

For help in creating your own low-cholesterol specialties, consult our features on recipe development (page 76) and makeovers (page 52). You'll also find plenty of useful tips in the Appendix beginning on page 98: a glossary, the American Heart Association Diet, a table listing the nutritional value of a number of foods, herb and spice suggestions, a substitution list, an explanation of how to read food labels, and a table of desirable weights.

Who should follow a low-cholesterol diet?

The American Heart Association offers specific diet plans for people who have been advised to reduce their blood cholesterol level. But both the AHA and the National Institutes of Health advise every adult to follow a lowfat, low-cholesterol eating plan. Of course, you should consult your physician whenever you begin a new diet or exercise program. If your doctor hasn't recommended any particular regimen, you can enthusiastically add our recipes to your diet; they're both healthful and delicious. We've tested them on adults and children whose concerns range from healthy hearts to happy tastebuds.

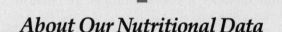

About Our Nutritional Data

For our recipes, we provide a nutritional analysis stating calorie count (percentage of fat, carbohydrates, and protein); grams of total fat and saturated fat; milligrams of cholesterol; grams of carbohydrates and protein; and milligrams of sodium. Generally, the nutritional information applies to a single serving, based on the largest number of servings given for each recipe.

The nutritional analysis does not include optional ingredients or those for which no specific amount is stated. If an ingredient is listed with an option, the information was calculated using the first choice. Likewise, if a range is given for the amount of an ingredient, values were figured based on the first, lower amount.

Here's proof positive that you can limit your intake of fat and cholesterol and still enjoy a wealth of fruits, vegetables, pasta, grains, legumes, breads, lean meats, poultry, fish, and lowfat dairy products. Cook to your heart's content!

Soups

Soups are part of the secret to successful low-cholesterol

eating. Stock up the broth with pasta, grains, legumes,

fruits, and vegetables, add your choice of poultry, seafood,

meat, or dairy products, and enjoy a satisfying bowlful

that's rich in carbohydrates and protein.

Soups can serve as a single course or a one-bowl meal.

They can announce or round off an entrée; they can

begin or end a day. There are even soups to suit each

season. Take your pick from the choices in this chapter—

you'll satisfy your appetite as well as your health goals.

Beef & Vegetable Soup

Per serving:

220 calories (30% fat, 25% carbohydrates, 45% protein),
7 g total fat, 2 g saturated fat, 56 mg cholesterol,
14 g carbohydrates, 25 g protein, 1067 mg sodium

Preparation time: About 15 minutes

Cooking time: About 3½ hours

The more blustery the weather, the better this soup tastes. Celery, carrots, tomatoes, and tender steak mingle in a rich broth; some of the cooked vegetables are puréed to thicken the soup.

- 2 pounds lean bottom round steak
- 1 to 2 pounds soup bones (optional)
- 8 cups regular-strength beef broth
- 3 cups water
- 1 cup dry white wine
- 1 can (15 oz.) stewed tomatoes
- 1 large onion, chopped
- 1 pound carrots, thinly sliced
- 6 stalks celery, thinly sliced
- ½ cup chopped parsley
- 4 cloves garlic, minced or pressed
- 1 bay leaf
- ½ teaspoon *each* dry basil, dry rosemary, and dry thyme leaves
  Grated Parmesan cheese (optional)

In an 8- to 10-quart pan, cook steak over medium-high heat until well browned on both sides. Add soup bones, if desired. Stir in broth, water, wine, tomatoes, onion, carrots, celery, parsley, garlic, bay leaf, basil, rosemary, and thyme. Bring to a boil; then reduce heat, cover, and simmer until meat is very tender when pierced (about 3 hours). Lift out and discard soup bones, if used. Lift out steak; when steak is cool enough to handle, trim off fat and cut meat into bite-size pieces.

Pour broth through a fine strainer into a bowl; skim off and discard fat. Discard bay leaf. Whirl half the vegetables in a food processor or blender until coarsely puréed. Return purée, remaining vegetables, meat, and broth to pan. (At this point, you may cover and refrigerate for up to 1 day; remove any additional fat before reheating.)

To serve, bring soup to a boil over high heat, stirring often. Ladle into bowls. Offer cheese to sprinkle over individual portions, if desired. Makes 6 to 8 servings.

Double Pea Soup

Per serving:

467 calories (10% fat, 63% carbohydrates, 27% protein),
6 g total fat, .4 g saturated fat, 0 mg cholesterol,
76 g carbohydrates, 32 g protein, 1337 mg sodium

Preparation time: About 10 minutes

Cooking time: About 1 hour

Thick pea soup warms up Sunday supper. Start with lightly sautéed garlic, chicken broth, and dried split peas; at the last minute, add tiny green peas to the simmering pot for extra color and texture.

- 2 pounds dried yellow or green split peas
- 1 tablespoon margarine
- 4 cloves garlic, minced
- 10 cups regular-strength chicken broth or Chicken-Vegetable Stock (page 76)
- 1 package (10 oz.) frozen tiny peas

Sort split peas to remove any debris. Rinse and drain split peas; set aside.

Melt margarine in a 5- to 6-quart pan over medium-high heat; add garlic and stir until golden (about 2 minutes). Add split peas and broth; increase heat to high and bring to a boil. Reduce heat, cover, and simmer until peas are tender when mashed (about 45 minutes). Add frozen peas and continue to simmer, stirring often, until hot (about 5 more minutes). If made ahead, let cool, then cover and refrigerate for up to 3 days (freeze for longer storage). Reheat to serve. Makes 8 servings.

Triple your chances to please Mom and eat your spinach! Tortellini & Chicken Soup (recipe on facing page) features cheese-filled spinach pasta and chopped fresh spinach in a meaty chicken broth. Mini-calzones (recipe on page 12), tiny whole wheat turnovers stuffed with spinach and ham, complete the meal.

Tortellini & Chicken Soup

Per serving:
181 **calories** *(26% fat, 38% carbohydrates, 36% protein),*
6 g **total fat**, *.2 g* **saturated fat**, *22 mg* **cholesterol**,
18 g **carbohydrates**, *17 g* **protein**, *1628 mg* **sodium**

Preparation time: About 10 minutes

Cooking time: About 15 minutes

Here's a soup with everything—meat, rice, vegetables, even cheese-filled spinach pasta. Let diners add Parmesan cheese to taste.

- 4½ **quarts or 3 cans (49 ½ oz.** *each***) regular-strength chicken broth**
- 1 **package (9 oz.) fresh cheese-filled spinach tortellini**
- 1 **pound spinach, rinsed well, stems removed, and leaves coarsely chopped**
- 1 **pound skinned and boned chicken breast, cut into ½-inch chunks**
- ½ **pound mushrooms, sliced**
- 1 **medium-size red bell pepper, seeded and diced**
- 1 **cup cooked rice**
- 2 **teaspoons dry tarragon leaves Grated Parmesan cheese (optional)**

In an 8- to 10-quart pan, bring broth to a boil, covered, over high heat. Add tortellini, reduce heat, and boil gently, uncovered, just until tender to bite (about 6 minutes).

Add spinach, chicken, mushrooms, bell pepper, rice, and tarragon to broth; return to a boil over high heat. Reduce heat, cover, and simmer until chicken is no longer pink in center; cut to test (about 2 minutes). Ladle soup into large bowls. Offer cheese to sprinkle over individual portions, if desired. Makes 10 to 12 servings.

Curried Fish Chowder

Per serving:
246 **calories** *(23% fat, 44% carbohydrates, 33% protein),*
6 g **total fat**, *1 g* **saturated fat**, *29 mg* **cholesterol**,
28 g **carbohydrates**, *21 g* **protein**, *1120 mg* **sodium**

Preparation time: About 15 minutes

Cooking time: About 35 minutes

Add a little zest to traditional fish chowder: season it with curry powder, fresh ginger, and hot chiles. Green onions and tangy yogurt top this one-bowl entrée.

- 1 **tablespoon margarine**
- 1 **large onion, chopped**
- 2 **tablespoons minced fresh ginger**
- 1 **clove garlic, minced or pressed**
- 1½ **tablespoons curry powder**
- 6 **cups regular-strength chicken broth or Chicken-Vegetable Stock (page 76)**
- 1 **pound thin-skinned potatoes, unpeeled, cut into ½-inch cubes**
- ½ **pound carrots, cut into ½-inch cubes**
- 3 **strips (***each* **½ by 4 inches) lemon peel (yellow part only)**
- 2 **small dried hot red chiles**
- 1 **pound rockfish fillets, cut into ½-inch cubes**
- ¼ **cup thinly sliced green onions (including tops)**
- 1 **cup nonfat plain yogurt**
- 1 **lemon, cut into wedges**

Melt margarine in a 5- to 6-quart pan over medium-high heat. Add chopped onion, ginger, and garlic; cook, stirring occasionally, until onion is soft (about 7 minutes). Add curry powder; stir for 2 minutes. Add broth, potatoes, carrots, lemon peel, and chiles; bring to a boil over high heat. Reduce heat, cover, and simmer until potatoes are tender when pierced (about 20 minutes).

Add fish. Cover and simmer until fish is opaque (about 2 minutes). If desired, remove and discard chiles. Ladle soup into a tureen and sprinkle with green onions; top with yogurt. Serve with lemon wedges. Makes 4 to 6 servings.

Appetizers

Pictured on page 10
Mini-calzones

Tiny spinach-stuffed turnovers made with whole wheat pizza dough are perfect party fare. You can even bake them a day ahead, then reheat just before serving.

> Whole Wheat Dough (recipe follows)
> 2 tablespoons olive oil
> 2 tablespoons minced shallot
> 2 ounces Black Forest ham, chopped
> 4 cups coarsely chopped, lightly packed spinach
> ¼ cup part-skim ricotta cheese
> ½ teaspoon ground nutmeg

Prepare Whole Wheat Dough. While dough is rising, prepare filling. Heat 1 tablespoon of the oil in a 10- to 12-inch frying pan over medium-high heat. Add shallot and ham; cook, stirring occasionally, until shallot is soft (about 7 minutes). Add spinach and cook until liquid has evaporated (about 5 minutes). Remove from heat. Add ricotta cheese and nutmeg; mix well. Let cool.

Punch down dough and shape into a ball. On a lightly floured board, roll dough into a circle ⅛ inch thick. Using a 3-inch cookie cutter, cut out circles. Place about 1 teaspoon of the spinach filling on each circle. Fold dough over filling; press edges together to seal. Transfer to a greased, cornmeal-dusted baking sheet. Brush tops lightly with remaining 1 tablespoon oil; with a fork, prick tops.

The party isn't over just because you've decided to switch to a low-cholesterol, lowfat diet: you can still treat yourself and your guests to a variety of appetizers. When you serve our Mini-calzones, moist Chicken Yakitori, and Layered Bean Dip, there's no need to mention that they're healthful—unless you want to brag a bit! Just enjoy and let the party begin.

Bake in a 425° oven until lightly browned (about 15 minutes). Serve warm. If made ahead, let cool, then cover and refrigerate for up to 1 day. To reheat, arrange on baking sheets and heat in a 425° oven for about 5 minutes. Makes 3 dozen calzones.

Whole Wheat Dough. In a large bowl, combine 1 package **active dry yeast** and ¾ cup **warm water** (about 110°F); let stand until softened (about 5 minutes). Add 1 teaspoon *each* **salt** and **sugar** and 1 cup **all-purpose flour**. Beat until smooth. Using a heavy-duty mixer or a wooden spoon, beat in about 1 cup **whole wheat flour** or enough to make dough hold together. Turn out onto a lightly floured board and knead until dough is smooth and elastic (about 5 minutes), adding more flour as needed to prevent sticking. Place in an oiled bowl and turn over to grease top; cover and let rise in a warm place until almost doubled in bulk (about 1 hour). Then roll out and cut as directed.

■

Per calzone: 38 calories (27% fat, 57% carbohydrates, 16% protein), 1 g total fat, .2 g saturated fat, 1 mg cholesterol, 6 g carbohydrates, 2 g protein, 104 mg sodium

---

Pictured on page 1
Chicken Yakitori

Thread chicken chunks and green onions on skewers and marinate briefly in a soy-sherry blend, then grill over low coals. The result is as delicious as it's enjoyable to eat.

> ½ cup *each* soy sauce and cream sherry
> 3 tablespoons sugar
> 2 pounds skinned and boned chicken breasts, cut into bite-size pieces
> 4 bunches green onions (including tops), cut into 1½-inch lengths

Soak sixteen 6-inch bamboo skewers in warm water to cover for 30 minutes.

In a pan, combine soy, sherry, and sugar. Bring to a boil over high heat; reduce heat and simmer, uncovered, for 3 minutes. Pour into a 9- by 13-inch dish and set aside.

Thread chicken and onions on skewers, alternating chicken with onion pieces on each skewer. Place in soy marinade, turn to coat, and let stand for 15 minutes.

Lift skewers from marinade and drain briefly (reserve marinade). Place skewers on a lightly greased grill 4 to 6 inches above a solid bed of low coals. Cook, basting with marinade and turning as needed to brown evenly, until meat is no longer pink in center; cut to test (about 10 minutes). Makes 16 skewers.

■

Per skewer: 90 calories (8% fat, 28% carbohydrates, 64% protein), .8 g total fat, .2 g saturated fat, 33 mg cholesterol, 6 g carbohydrates, 14 g protein, 554 mg sodium

Layered Bean Dip

Hummus, the Mideast chick pea spread, is topped with yogurt, cucumber, radishes, and feta cheese for a multilevel dip. Scoop it up with crunchy Pita Crisps.

>   **Pita Crisps (recipe follows)**
> 1 **can (about 1 lb.) garbanzo beans, drained (reserve ¼ cup liquid)**
> 3 **tablespoons tahini (sesame-seed paste)**
> ¼ **cup lemon juice**
> ½ **teaspoon ground cumin**
> 1 **clove garlic, minced or pressed**
> ½ **cup nonfat plain yogurt**
> 1 **tablespoon minced fresh mint leaves**
> ½ **cup *each* thinly sliced cucumber and thinly sliced radishes**
> ¼ **cup crumbled feta cheese**
>   **Fresh mint sprigs**

Prepare Pita Crisps; set aside.

In a food processor or blender, whirl beans, the reserved ¼ cup liquid, tahini, lemon juice, cumin, and garlic until smooth. On a large platter, spread mixture out to make an 8-inch-diameter circle.

Mix yogurt and minced mint; spread evenly over beans. Sprinkle cucumber, radishes, and cheese over yogurt mixture. Garnish with mint sprigs. Tuck Pita Crisps around edge of dip; scoop dip onto crisps to eat. Makes 12 servings.

Pita Crisps. Split apart 6 **pocket breads** (*each* 6 inches in diameter) to make 12 rounds. Mix 3 tablespoons **olive oil** with 1 clove **garlic,** minced or pressed. Brush split sides of bread with oil mixture and sprinkle with freshly ground **pepper.** Cut each round into 6 wedges. Place in a single layer on baking sheets. Bake in a 400° oven until crisp and golden (about 5 minutes). Serve at room temperature. Makes 6 dozen crisps.

Per serving: 199 calories (30% fat, 58% carbohydrates, 12% protein), 7 g total fat, 1 g saturated fat, 3 mg cholesterol, 29 g carbohydrates, 6 g protein, 336 mg sodium

Pictured on page 31
Quick Cuke Chips

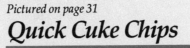

Cucumbers and red bell pepper strips marinated in dill-flavored vinegar are attractive as well as addictive.

> 3 **large cucumbers (about 2½ lbs. *total*), unpeeled**
> 1 **large red bell pepper, seeded and cut into ½-inch-wide strips**
> 1 **large onion, thinly sliced**
> 1 **tablespoon *each* salt and dill seeds**
> ¾ **cup sugar**
> ½ **cup white wine vinegar**

Cut cucumbers crosswise into ¼-inch slices. In a large bowl, combine cucumbers, bell pepper, and onion. Add salt and dill seeds; stir well. Let stand, uncovered, for 1 to 2 hours; stir occasionally.

In a small bowl, stir together sugar and vinegar until sugar is dissolved. Pour over vegetables and mix gently. Spoon into glass or ceramic containers, cover, and refrigerate for at least 1 day or up to 3 weeks. Drain before serving. Makes about 2 quarts.

Per ¼ cup: 26 calories (3% fat, 93% carbohydrates, 4% protein), .1 g total fat, 0 g saturated fat, 0 mg cholesterol, 6 g carbohydrates, .3 g protein, 207 mg sodium

Oysters with Tomatillo Salsa

A tangy salsa made with tomatillos, green chiles, and lime juice is just the right complement for grilled oysters hot off the barbecue. Make the salsa up to 2 days ahead, if you like.

>   **Tomatillo Salsa (recipe follows)**
> 48 **small Pacific oysters in shells (*each* 2 to 3 inches in diameter)**

Prepare Tomatillo Salsa; set aside.

Scrub oysters with a stiff brush under cool running water. Then set oysters, cupped sides down, on a grill 4 to 6 inches above a solid bed of hot coals. When shells begin to open, carefully remove oysters from grill; shells and juices are hot, so use tongs or hot pads. Cut oysters free from shells, discarding top shells.

To serve, spoon 1 tablespoon salsa over each oyster; serve oysters in the shell. Makes 4 dozen appetizers.

Tomatillo Salsa. Drain 2 cans (13 oz. *each*) **tomatillos** and discard juice. Chop tomatillos, place in a large bowl, and mix in 1 can (4 oz.) **diced green chiles,** ½ cup *each* minced **green onions** (including tops) and minced **fresh cilantro** (coriander), and 2 tablespoons **lime juice.** Season to taste with **salt.** If made ahead, cover and refrigerate for up to 2 days. Makes 3 cups.

Per appetizer: 34 calories (25% fat, 30% carbohydrates, 45% protein), 1 g total fat; .2 g saturated fat; 21 mg cholesterol; 3 g carbohydrates; 4 g protein; 54 mg sodium

Spiced Cream of Pumpkin Soup

Preparation time: About 15 minutes

Cooking time: About 40 minutes

Celebrate autumn's arrival with a smooth, lightly spiced soup flavored with leeks—the mild-mannered member of the onion family. Sautéed leeks, sliced carrots, colorful pumpkin, and a handful of sweet currants combine in chicken broth; the finished soup is topped with toasted pumpkin seeds.

    3 large leeks (about 1 lb. *total*)
    1 tablespoon olive oil or salad oil
    ½ cup currants
    ½ pound carrots, thinly sliced
    3 cups regular-strength chicken broth or Chicken-Vegetable Stock (page 76)
    2 cups nonfat milk
    1 can (1 lb.) solid-pack pumpkin
    ¼ teaspoon ground nutmeg
      Toasted pumpkin seeds

Per serving:
*165 **calories** (20% fat, 66% carbohydrates, 14% protein),*
*4 g **total fat**, .5 g **saturated fat**, 2 mg **cholesterol**,*
*29 g **carbohydrates**, 6 g **protein**, 570 mg **sodium***

Trim ends and all but 3 inches of green tops from leeks; remove tough outer leaves. Split leeks lengthwise; rinse well, then thinly slice crosswise. Set aside.

Heat oil in a 3- to 4-quart pan over medium heat; add currants and stir until puffed (about 2 minutes). Lift from pan with a slotted spoon; set aside. Add leeks and carrots to pan; stir often until leeks are golden (about 10 minutes). Add 1 cup of the broth; bring to a boil, then reduce heat, cover, and simmer until carrots are very tender to bite (about 10 minutes).

In a blender or food processor, whirl leek mixture until smooth. Return to pan and add remaining 2 cups broth, milk, pumpkin, and nutmeg. Cook over medium heat, stirring often, until soup is hot (about 15 minutes). Stir in currants. Offer pumpkin seeds to add to taste. Makes 6 servings.

Cantaloupe-Tangerine Soup

Preparation time: About 10 minutes

Here's a summertime soup you can serve at breakfast, lunch, or dinner! Tangy tangerine juice blended with sweet cantaloupe is a refreshing beginning or cool, soothing finish to your day.

    1 large cantaloupe (about 3 lbs.), chilled
    1 can (6 oz.) frozen concentrated tangerine or orange juice, partially thawed
      Fresh mint sprigs

Per serving:
*146 **calories** (4% fat, 90% carbohydrates, 6% protein),*
*.7 g **total fat**, 0 g **saturated fat**, 0 mg **cholesterol**,*
*35 g **carbohydrates**, 2 g **protein**, 17 mg **sodium***

Cut cantaloupe in half; scoop out and discard seeds. Scoop flesh from shell and place in a blender or food processor; add tangerine juice and whirl until smoothly puréed. If desired, cover and refrigerate for up to 24 hours; whirl again to blend before serving. Pour soup into bowls; garnish with mint sprigs. Makes 4 servings.

When frosty weather arrives, sit down to a bowl of Spiced Cream of Pumpkin Soup (recipe on facing page). Toasted pumpkin seeds and currants plus carrots and leeks add extra flavor and texture. Accompany the soup with a loaf of Raisin Pumpernickel Bread (recipe on page 83).

Poultry, Seafood & Meats

Does meat have to disappear from a low-cholesterol diet?

Not if you choose the type of meat, portion size, and

cooking method wisely.

Poultry, fish, and red meat all contain about the same

amount of cholesterol; the difference lies in the saturated fat

content. To minimize fat calories, our recipes concentrate on

white meat of turkey and chicken, fish, and leaner cuts of red

meat. Cooking techniques are lowfat, too—we broil, bake,

barbecue, poach, and stir-fry. You'll see how easy it is

to get the benefits of meat—complete protein, iron, and

B vitamins—without stocking up on saturated fat.

Chicken Breasts with Blueberries

Per serving:
290 calories (18% fat, 45% carbohydrates, 37% protein), 6 g total fat, .8 g saturated fat, 66 mg cholesterol, 33 g carbohydrates, 27 g protein, 416 mg sodium

Preparation time: About 5 minutes

Cooking time: About 30 minutes

Here's a chicken dish with a difference—blueberries! The fruit is mixed with apricot jam and mustard for a tangy sauce. Because the recipe uses frozen berries, you can make this entrée all year round.

- **2 whole chicken breasts, skinned, boned, and split (1 lb. meat *total*)**
- **1 tablespoon salad oil**
- **½ cup apricot jam**
- **3 tablespoons Dijon mustard**
- **½ cup frozen unsweetened blueberries**
- **⅓ cup white wine vinegar**
  Watercress sprigs

Rinse chicken and pat dry. Heat oil in a 10- to 12-inch frying pan over medium-high heat. Add chicken; cook, turning as needed, until browned on both sides (about 6 minutes).

Meanwhile, in a small bowl, stir together jam and mustard. Spread jam mixture over tops of browned breasts; sprinkle with blueberries. Reduce heat to medium-low, cover, and cook until meat is no longer pink in thickest part; cut to test (about 15 minutes). With a slotted spoon, lift chicken and blueberries to a platter; keep warm.

Add vinegar to pan, increase heat to high, and bring to a boil. Boil, stirring occasionally, until sauce is reduced by a third and thickened (about 5 minutes). Pour sauce over chicken; garnish with watercress. Makes 4 servings.

Plum Chicken

Per serving:
353 calories (4% fat, 65% carbohydrates, 31% protein), 2 g total fat, .4 g saturated fat, 66 mg cholesterol, 58 g carbohydrates, 27 g protein, 243 mg sodium

Preparation time: About 10 minutes

Baking time: About 25 minutes

Baked in a spicy, ginger-sparked plum sauce, these moist, richly glazed chicken breasts are easy to prepare.

- **2 whole chicken breasts, skinned, boned, and split (1 lb. meat *total*)**
- **1 cup Oriental plum sauce**
- **¼ cup minced onion**
- **2 tablespoons lemon juice**
- **1 tablespoon reduced-sodium soy sauce**
- **1 teaspoon grated lemon peel**
- **½ teaspoon *each* dry mustard and ground ginger**
- **¼ teaspoon *each* pepper and liquid hot pepper seasoning**
- **¼ teaspoon anise seeds, crushed**

Rinse chicken, pat dry, and place, skinned side up, in a 9- by 13-inch baking dish or other shallow 3-quart baking dish. In a small bowl, stir together plum sauce, onion, lemon juice, soy, lemon peel, mustard, ginger, pepper, hot pepper seasoning, and anise seeds. Pour over chicken.

Bake chicken, uncovered, in a 400° oven until meat is no longer pink in thickest part; cut to test (about 25 minutes). Baste chicken halfway through baking. To serve, lift chicken to a platter; spoon sauce on top. Makes 4 servings.

*For the centerpiece of a special dinner, choose cheese-covered Broccoli-stuffed
Chicken Breasts (recipe on facing page). Tender meat wraps around
a rich-tasting filling flavored with shallots and Madeira.
Sweet young vegetables—baby carrots, tiny potatoes, and summer squash—
complete the meal beautifully.*

Pictured on facing page

Broccoli-stuffed Chicken Breasts

Per serving:
*236 **calories** (28% fat, 16% carbohydrates, 56% protein),*
*7 g **total fat**, 3 g **saturated fat**, 76 mg **cholesterol**,*
*9 g **carbohydrates**, 33 g **protein**, 158 mg **sodium***

Preparation time: About 45 minutes

Baking & broiling time: About 17 minutes

Topped with Swiss cheese and stuffed with bright green broccoli, chicken breasts slice beautifully for a party plate. Shallots, mushrooms, and Madeira add a French flavor to the filling.

- 1 **tablespoon salad oil**
- ½ **cup minced shallots**
- 1 **pound mushrooms, minced**
- 2 **cups broccoli flowerets**
- 2 **tablespoons Madeira**
- 2 **tablespoons grated Parmesan cheese**
- ½ **cup shredded Swiss cheese**
- 3 **whole chicken breasts, skinned, boned, and split (1½ lbs. meat *total*)**

Heat oil in a 10- to 12-inch frying pan over medium heat. Add shallots and mushrooms; cook, stirring occasionally, until shallots are soft (about 5 minutes). Add broccoli and Madeira, cover, and cook, stirring occasionally, until broccoli is tender-crisp to bite (about 5 minutes). Remove from heat and stir in Parmesan cheese and ¼ cup of the Swiss cheese; let cool.

Rinse chicken; pat dry. Place each breast half between 2 sheets of plastic wrap. Pound with a flat-surfaced mallet to a thickness of about ¼ inch.

In center of each breast half, mound an equal portion of the broccoli mixture. Roll chicken around filling to enclose. Set filled breasts, seam side down, in a greased 9- by 13-inch baking pan. Sprinkle with remaining ¼ cup Swiss cheese.

Bake, uncovered, in a 450° oven until meat is no longer pink and filling is hot in center; cut to test (about 15 minutes). Then broil chicken 4 to 6 inches below heat until cheese is browned (about 2 minutes). Makes 6 servings.

Stuffed Chicken Breasts with Chutney

Per serving:
*174 **calories** (18% fat, 18% carbohydrates, 64% protein),*
*3 g **total fat**, .6 g **saturated fat**, 66 mg **cholesterol**,*
*8 g **carbohydrates**, 27 g **protein**, 107 mg **sodium***

Preparation time: About 35 minutes

Cooking time: About 15 minutes

Flavored with lightly sautéed onions and garlic, this spinach filling is good enough to eat alone—but it's even better rolled inside chicken breasts and simmered in a simple sauce of broth, balsamic vinegar, and chutney.

- 1 **tablespoon olive oil**
- 2 **cloves garlic, minced or pressed**
- 1 **large onion, chopped**
- 2¼ **cups chopped spinach leaves**
- 4 **whole chicken breasts, skinned, boned, and split (2 lbs. meat *total*)**
- 1 **tablespoon balsamic vinegar**
- ½ **cup low-sodium chicken broth**
- ¼ **cup chutney**

Heat oil in a 12- to 14-inch frying pan over medium-high heat. Add garlic and onion and cook, stirring occasionally, until onion is soft (about 7 minutes). Add 2 cups of the spinach; let cool.

Rinse chicken; pat dry. Place each breast half between 2 sheets of plastic wrap. Pound with a flat-surfaced mallet to a thickness of about ¼ inch.

In center of each breast half, mound an equal portion of the spinach mixture. Roll meat around filling to enclose; fasten with wooden picks. Place chicken rolls in pan used for spinach.

In a small bowl, mix vinegar, broth, and chutney. Pour over chicken. Bring to a simmer over medium heat. Cover and simmer until meat is no longer pink and filling is hot in center; cut to test (about 8 minutes). Remove chicken from pan; remove wooden picks and keep chicken warm.

Increase heat to high and bring chutney mixture to a boil. Cook, stirring occasionally, until reduced to ½ cup (about 5 minutes); then pour over chicken. Garnish with remaining ¼ cup spinach. Makes 8 servings.

Garlicky Broiled Chicken

Per serving:
213 calories (30% fat, 17% carbohydrates, 53% protein), 7 g total fat, 1 g saturated fat, 66 mg cholesterol, 9 g carbohydrates, 29 g protein, 83 mg sodium

Preparation time: About 10 minutes

Marinating time: At least 2 hours

Cooking time: About 20 minutes

Broiled chicken breasts are sometimes boringly bland—but not these! The garlicky marinade will really wake up your tastebuds.

- ⅓ **cup lemon juice**
- 2 **tablespoons olive oil**
- ⅓ **cup dry white wine**
- 6 **cloves garlic, minced or pressed**
- 2 **bay leaves, crumbled**
- 2 **whole chicken breasts, skinned, boned, and split (1 lb. meat *total*)**
- 2 **large red bell peppers, seeded and cut into 1½-inch squares**
- ¾ **pound medium-size mushrooms, halved**

In a shallow bowl, stir together lemon juice, oil, wine, garlic, and bay leaves. Rinse and drain chicken; add to marinade and turn to coat. Cover and refrigerate for at least 2 hours or up to 1 day, turning chicken occasionally.

Lift chicken from marinade; reserve marinade. Place chicken on a rack in a broiler pan. Broil 4 inches below heat for 15 minutes, basting with marinade and turning as needed to cook evenly. Arrange bell peppers and mushrooms alongside chicken, baste lightly, and continue to broil until chicken is no longer pink in thickest part; cut to test (about 5 more minutes). Makes 4 servings.

Chicken Picadillo

Per serving:
365 calories (21% fat, 44% carbohydrates, 35% protein), 9 g total fat, 1 g saturated fat, 66 mg cholesterol, 40 g carbohydrates, 32 g protein, 401 mg sodium

Preparation time: About 45 minutes

Baking time: About 1½ hours

This oven-baked stew boasts sunny colors and spicy flavors from Latin America.

- 1 **tablespoon olive oil**
- 1½ **pounds skinned and boned chicken breasts, cut into 1½-inch chunks**
- 1 **large onion, chopped**
- 2 **cloves garlic, minced or pressed**
- 1 **medium-size green bell pepper, seeded and chopped**
- 1 **large can (15 oz.) no-salt-added tomato sauce**
- 1 **cup dry white wine**
- 1 **fresh jalapeño chile, thinly sliced**
- 1½ **teaspoons dry oregano leaves**
- 1 **teaspoon dry thyme leaves**
- 1½ **pounds small red thin-skinned potatoes (*each* 1½ to 2 inches in diameter), unpeeled, quartered**
- ½ **cup *each* pimento-stuffed green olives, thinly sliced, and raisins**
- 1 **cup frozen peas, thawed**
- ¼ **cup slivered blanched almonds**

Heat oil in a 12- to 14-inch frying pan over medium heat. Add chicken and cook, stirring often, until browned on all sides (about 6 minutes). Transfer chicken to a 4- to 5-quart casserole.

Add onion, garlic, and bell pepper to pan; cook, stirring occasionally, until onion is soft (about 10 minutes). Add tomato sauce, wine, chile, oregano, and thyme; cook, stirring occasionally, until sauce comes to a boil. Boil gently, uncovered, for 5 minutes.

Pour sauce over chicken; add potatoes, olives, and raisins. Cover and bake in a 375° oven until potatoes are tender when pierced (about 1½ hours). Stir in peas and almonds. Makes 6 servings.

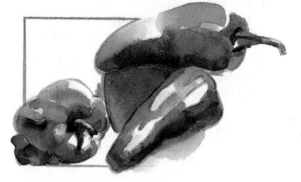

Chicken & Fruit Kebabs

Per serving:

277 calories (27% fat, 33% carbohydrates, 40% protein), 9 g total fat, 1 g saturated fat, 66 mg cholesterol, 23 g carbohydrates, 28 g protein, 464 mg sodium

Preparation time: About 45 minutes

Marinating time: At least 1 hour

Grilling time: About 10 minutes

Set up your barbecue and savor these kebabs of chicken chunks marinated in sherry and soy, paired perfectly with fresh pineapple and papaya.

Sherry-Soy Marinade (recipe follows)

2 **tablespoons sesame seeds**

1½ **pounds skinned and boned chicken breasts, cut into 1½-inch chunks**

1 **large papaya (about 1¼ lbs.), peeled, seeded, and cut into 1½-inch chunks**

1 **small pineapple (about 2½ lbs.), peeled, cored, and cut into 1½-inch chunks**

Prepare Sherry-Soy Marinade and set aside.

In a small frying pan, toast sesame seeds over medium heat until golden (about 3 minutes), shaking pan frequently. Set aside.

Combine chicken and ¼ cup of the marinade in a shallow bowl; mix gently to coat (reserve remaining marinade). Cover and let stand at room temperature for 1 hour (or refrigerate for up to 8 hours).

If using bamboo skewers, soak 12 skewers in hot water to cover for 30 minutes. Lift chicken from marinade and drain briefly (discard marinade left in bowl). Thread chicken equally on 6 bamboo or metal skewers. Thread fruit on 6 more skewers, alternating papaya and pineapple on each skewer.

Place chicken on a lightly greased grill 4 to 6 inches above a solid bed of hot coals. Cook, turning occasionally, until meat is no longer pink in center; cut to test (about 10 minutes).

Meanwhile, brush fruit with a little of the reserved marinade. Place on grill next to chicken and cook, turning occasionally, just until heated through and lightly browned (about 3 minutes).

Sprinkle chicken and fruit with some of the reserved marinade, then with sesame seeds. Accompany with any remaining marinade. Makes 6 servings.

Sherry-Soy Marinade. In a small bowl, stir together ⅓ cup **dry sherry,** 3 tablespoons *each* **soy sauce** and **Oriental sesame oil,** and 1½ teaspoons finely minced **fresh ginger.**

Chicken-stuffed Melon with Raspberries

Per serving:

340 calories (6% fat, 61% carbohydrates, 33% protein), 3 g total fat, .5 g saturated fat, 66 mg cholesterol, 55 g carbohydrates, 29 g protein, 101 mg sodium

Preparation time: About 25 minutes, plus 20 minutes to cook chicken

Whenever a recipe calls for cooked chicken breasts, try steeping the meat for extra moistness.

Lime-Honey Dressing (recipe follows)

1½ **pounds skinned and boned chicken breasts**

4 **cups water**

2 **large cantaloupes (about 3 lbs.** *each***)**

1 **cup seedless green grapes**

2 **kiwi fruit, peeled and sliced**

1 **cup raspberries**

Prepare dressing; set aside. Rinse and drain chicken. In a 4- to 5-quart pan, bring water to a boil over high heat. Add chicken, cover pan, and remove from heat. Let stand, covered, until chicken is no longer pink in thickest part; cut to test (about 20 minutes). Drain chicken and place in ice water until cool; drain again. Cut into ½-inch chunks.

Cut each cantaloupe in half, making zigzag cuts. Scoop out and discard seeds. With a curved grapefruit knife, cut fruit from rind, then cut into ½-inch chunks. Drain melon pieces and shells.

In a bowl, combine melon, chicken, and grapes; spoon into shells. Top with kiwi slices, raspberries, and dressing. Makes 4 servings.

Lime-Honey Dressing. Stir together ½ cup *each* **lime juice** and **honey** with ½ teaspoon *each* **ground coriander** and **ground nutmeg.**

Chicken Jambalaya

Per serving:

*471 **calories** (16% fat, 49% carbohydrates, 35% protein), 8 g **total fat**, 2 g **saturated fat**, 85 mg **cholesterol**, 57 g **carbohydrates**, 42 g **protein**, 685 mg **sodium***

Preparation time: About 45 minutes

Baking time: About 45 minutes

Seasoned with plenty of red pepper, jambalaya is definitely not for timid tastes! Cubed chicken and smoky Canadian bacon bake with rice, tomatoes, onion, and bell peppers in this Cajun specialty.

- 1 **tablespoon salad oil**
- ½ **pound Canadian bacon, diced**
- 1½ **pounds skinned and boned chicken breasts, cut into bite-size chunks**
- 1 **large onion, chopped**
- 3 **cloves garlic, minced or pressed**
- 2 **large green bell peppers, seeded and chopped**
- 1 **cup chopped celery**
- 6 **large tomatoes (about 2 lbs. *total*), chopped**
- 1 **large can (15 oz.) no-salt-added tomato sauce**
- 2 **bay leaves, crumbled**
- 1 **teaspoon dry thyme leaves**
- 2 **teaspoons ground white pepper**
- 1 **teaspoon ground red pepper (cayenne)**
- ½ **cup chopped parsley**
- 1½ **cups long-grain white rice**
- 3 **cups low-sodium chicken broth**

Heat oil in a 12- to 14-inch frying pan over medium heat. Add Canadian bacon and chicken; cook, stirring often, until browned on all sides (about 6 minutes). Transfer chicken to a 4- to 5-quart casserole.

Add onion, garlic, bell peppers, and celery to pan. Cook, stirring occasionally, until onion is soft (about 10 minutes). Add tomatoes, tomato sauce, bay leaves, thyme, white pepper, red pepper, and parsley; cook, stirring occasionally, until sauce boils. Boil gently, uncovered, for 5 minutes.

Pour sauce over chicken; stir in rice and broth. Cover and bake in a 375° oven until rice is tender to bite (about 45 minutes). Makes 6 servings.

Couscous Chicken

Per serving:

*318 **calories** (10% fat, 47% carbohydrates, 43% protein), 3 g **total fat**, .5 g **saturated fat**, 67 mg **cholesterol**, 38 g **carbohydrates**, 35 g **protein**, 808 mg **sodium***

Preparation time: About 20 minutes, plus 30 minutes to cook chicken and couscous

Chilling time: At least 1 hour

On a warm evening, enjoy this hearty cold salad of vegetables, chicken and couscous cooked in broth.

- 1½ **pounds skinned and boned chicken breasts**
- 4 **cups regular-strength chicken broth**
- 1 **cup couscous**
- ¼ **cup currants**
- 1 **tablespoon curry powder**
- ½ **teaspoon dry thyme leaves**
- 1 **package (9 oz.) frozen artichoke hearts, thawed and drained**
- ¼ **cup *each* chopped parsley and red onion**
- ¼ **pound carrots, shredded**
- 1 **medium-size red bell pepper, seeded and chopped**
- 1 **cup nonfat plain yogurt**
- 1 **tablespoon honey**
- 2 **cups cherry tomatoes**
- 6 **large lettuce leaves**

Rinse and drain chicken. In a 4- to 5-quart pan, bring broth to a boil over high heat. Add chicken, cover pan, and remove from heat. Let stand, covered, until chicken is no longer pink in thickest part; cut to test (about 20 minutes). Lift out chicken; reserve 2 cups of the broth.

In a 2- to 3-quart pan, bring reserved 2 cups broth to a boil. Stir in couscous, currants, curry powder, and thyme; return to a boil. Cover, remove from heat, and let stand until all liquid is absorbed (about 10 minutes); stir in artichokes.

Cut chicken into ½-inch chunks. Stir chicken, parsley, onion, carrots, and bell pepper into couscous. Mix yogurt and honey; add to couscous mixture with tomatoes. Cover; refrigerate for at least 1 hour or up to 1 day. Place a lettuce leaf on each of 6 plates; top with salad mixture. Makes 6 servings.

This Cajun casserole can warm up your party and your palate.
Hearty Chicken Jambalaya (recipe on facing page) tempts the tastebuds
with tender rice, chunks of chicken breast, and vegetables—and teases
with a generous dose of cayenne.

Lemon Turkey Scaloppine

Per serving:

*186 **calories** (26% fat, 16% carbohydrates, 58% protein),
5 g **total fat**, 1 g **saturated fat**, 70 mg **cholesterol**,
8 g **carbohydrates**, 27 g **protein**, 193 mg **sodium***

Preparation time: About 20 minutes

Cooking time: About 6 minutes

Looking for a lowfat alternative to veal for scaloppine? Try sliced turkey breast! Just cook it quickly to keep the meat moist and tender.

- 1 **pound skinned and boned turkey breast, sliced ½ inch thick**
- 2 **tablespoons all-purpose flour**
- 1 **tablespoon salad oil**
- ½ **cup lemon juice**
- 2 **tablespoons drained capers**
- 1 **lemon, thinly sliced**

Rinse turkey, pat dry, and cut into serving-size pieces. Place between sheets of plastic wrap. With a flat-surfaced mallet, pound turkey to a thickness of about ¼ inch. Dust with flour.

Heat oil in a 12- to 14-inch frying pan over medium-high heat. Add turkey and cook, turning once, until golden brown on both sides (about 4 minutes). With a slotted spoon, transfer turkey to a platter; keep warm.

Add lemon juice and capers to pan. Bring to a boil and cook, stirring, until thickened (about 2 minutes). Pour sauce over turkey; garnish with lemon slices. Makes 4 servings.

Turkey Chili

Per serving:

*407 **calories** (16% fat, 45% carbohydrates, 39% protein),
7 g **total fat**, 1 g **saturated fat**, 70 mg **cholesterol**,
47 g **carbohydrates**, 40 g **protein**, 1259 mg **sodium***

Preparation time: About 15 minutes

Cooking time: About 40 minutes

Tired of traditional chili? For an appetizing alternative, just substitute chunks of turkey for the beef; the dish is still spicy and thick with beans and tomatoes.

- 1 **tablespoon salad oil**
- 1 **pound skinned and boned turkey breast, cut into 1½-inch chunks**
- 1 **medium-size onion, chopped**
- 1 **small green bell pepper, seeded and chopped**
- 1 **clove garlic, minced or pressed**
- 1 **small can (about 8 oz.) tomatoes, drained and chopped**
- 2 **cans (about 15 oz. *each*) kidney beans, drained**
- 1 **large can (15 oz.) no-salt-added tomato sauce**
- 2 **tablespoons reduced-sodium soy sauce**
- 1½ **tablespoons chili powder**
- ½ **teaspoon *each* ground cumin, dry sage leaves, and dry thyme leaves**
- **Garnishes (optional; suggestions follow)**

Heat oil in a 12- to 14-inch frying pan over medium heat. Add turkey and cook, stirring often, until browned on all sides (about 6 minutes). Remove turkey from pan. Add onion, bell pepper, and garlic; cook, stirring occasionally, until onion is soft (about 10 minutes). Add tomatoes, beans, tomato sauce, soy, chili powder, cumin, sage, and thyme. Bring to a boil. Then reduce heat, cover, and simmer until chili is thick and meat is no longer pink in center; cut to test (about 20 minutes; uncover for last 5 minutes). Serve in bowls and accompany with garnishes. Makes 4 servings.

Garnishes. In separate bowls, offer 8 **green onions** (including tops), sliced; 1 cup chopped **tomatoes;** and ½ cup shredded **jack cheese,** if desired.

Turkey Curry with Soba

Per serving:
297 **calories** (21% fat, 44% carbohydrates, 35% protein),
7 g **total fat**, 1 g **saturated fat**, 48 mg **cholesterol**,
33 g **carbohydrates**, 26 g **protein**, 250 mg **sodium**

Preparation time: About 10 minutes

Cooking time: About 40 minutes

To make this dish, you mix up your own curry powder by blending a variety of spices. If you can't find soba noodles in the Asian foods section of your supermarket, you can substitute spaghettini.

- 1 **tablespoon salad oil**
- 1 **pound skinned and boned turkey breast, cut into 1½-inch chunks**
- 1 **large onion, thinly sliced**
- 1 **clove garlic, minced or pressed**
- 1 **tablespoon grated fresh ginger**
- 1 **teaspoon** *each* **crushed red pepper, ground coriander, ground cumin, and ground turmeric**
- ½ **teaspoon fennel seeds**
- 1 **cup regular-strength chicken broth**
- 1 **package (7 oz.) soba noodles**
- 1 **cup nonfat plain yogurt**
- ¼ **cup roasted unsalted cashews**

Heat oil in a 12- to 14-inch frying pan over medium heat. Add turkey and cook, stirring often, until browned on all sides (about 6 minutes). Remove from pan.

Add onion and garlic to pan; cook, stirring occasionally, until onion is soft (about 10 minutes). Add ginger, red pepper, coriander, cumin, turmeric, and fennel seeds; cook, stirring, for 1 minute.

Return turkey to pan. Add broth, reduce heat, cover, and simmer until meat is no longer pink in center; cut to test (about 20 minutes). Remove from heat.

While turkey is simmering, following package directions, cook noodles in boiling water until barely tender to bite; drain well. Place in a large, shallow serving bowl.

Stir yogurt into turkey mixture, then pour mixture over noodles. Garnish with cashews. Makes 4 to 6 servings.

Apple Turkey Loaf

Per serving:
228 **calories** (17% fat, 29% carbohydrates, 54% protein),
4 g **total fat**, 1 g **saturated fat**, 71 mg **cholesterol**,
16 g **carbohydrates**, 30 g **protein**, 190 mg **sodium**

Preparation time: About 25 minutes

Baking time: About 1 hour

Lightly blend spices and tart green apples with ground turkey breast for a lean, moist meat loaf that's delicious hot or cold.

- 1 **tablespoon margarine**
- 2 **tart green-skinned apples, such as Granny Smith, peeled, cored, and chopped**
- 1 **medium-size onion, chopped**
- 1½ **pounds ground skinned turkey breast**
- 1½ **teaspoons dry marjoram leaves**
- 1 **teaspoon** *each* **dry thyme leaves, dry sage leaves, and pepper**
- ½ **cup chopped parsley**
- 2 **egg whites**
- ½ **cup fine dry bread crumbs**
- ½ **cup nonfat milk**

Melt margarine in a 10- to 12-inch frying pan over medium heat. Add apples and onion. Cook, stirring occasionally, until onion is soft (about 10 minutes). Let cool, then scrape into a large bowl and mix in turkey, marjoram, thyme, sage, pepper, parsley, egg whites, bread crumbs, and milk. Pat mixture into a 5- by 9-inch loaf pan. Bake in a 350° oven until browned on top and no longer pink in center; cut to test (about 1 hour). Drain fat from loaf pan, then invert pan and turn loaf out onto a platter. Serve loaf hot; or let cool, then cover and refrigerate for up to 1 day. Makes 6 servings.

Pass your plate for a slice of Layered Turkey Enchiladas (recipe on facing page). The tower of tortillas encloses an appetizing mixture of ground turkey, salsa, fresh tomatoes, and cheese. Serve with simmered pinto beans and more salsa, if desired.

Layered Turkey Enchiladas

Per serving:

284 *calories* (29% fat, 35% carbohydrates, 36% protein), 9 g *total fat*, 4 g *saturated fat*, 67 mg *cholesterol*, 25 g *carbohydrates*, 26 g *protein*, 684 mg *sodium*

Preparation time: About 15 minutes

Baking time: About 1 hour and 20 minutes

Enchiladas are especially easy to prepare when you stack corn tortillas with the filling instead of rolling them around it.

    1 cup shredded extra-sharp Cheddar cheese
    1 pound ground skinned turkey breast
    1 large can (7 oz.) diced green chiles
    1 medium-size onion, chopped
    1 cup mild green salsa
    1½ cups chopped pear-shaped (Roma-type) tomatoes
    8 corn tortillas (*each* 6 to 7 inches in diameter)

Mix ¾ cup of the cheese with turkey, chiles, onion, ½ cup of the salsa, and 1 cup of the tomatoes. Divide into 7 equal portions.

Place 1 tortilla in a shallow 9- to 10-inch-diameter baking pan; cover evenly with one portion of the turkey mixture. Repeat to use remaining tortillas and turkey mixture; top stack with a tortilla. Cover with remaining ¼ cup cheese, ½ cup salsa, and ½ cup tomatoes.

Cover with foil and bake in a 400° oven for 40 minutes. Uncover and contiue to bake until turkey is no longer pink; cut to center of stack to test (about 40 more minutes). Let stand for 5 minutes, then cut into wedges. Makes 4 to 6 servings.

Minced Turkey in Lettuce

Per serving:

163 *calories* (20% fat, 30% carbohydrates, 50% protein), 4 g *total fat*, .6 g *saturated fat*, 47 mg *cholesterol*, 12 g *carbohydrates*, 20 g *protein*, 272 mg *sodium*

Preparation time: About 15 minutes, plus 30 minutes to soak mushrooms

Cooking time: About 7 minutes

Spoon this quick stir-fry of ground turkey and vegetables into lettuce cups, then eat it out of hand. If you like, accent the gingery turkey mixture with a little spicy hoisin sauce.

       Cooking Sauce (recipe follows)
    3 medium-size dried shiitake mushrooms (*each* about 2 inches in diameter)
    1 tablespoon salad oil
    2 cloves garlic, minced or pressed
    1½ teaspoons grated fresh ginger
    ½ teaspoon crushed red pepper
    1 pound ground skinned turkey breast
    1 can (about 8 oz.) sliced bamboo shoots, drained and minced
    1 can (about 8 oz.) water chestnuts, drained and minced
    6 green onions (including tops), minced
    ½ cup frozen peas, thawed
    12 large lettuce leaves
       Hoisin sauce (optional)

Prepare Cooking Sauce and set aside. Soak mushrooms in warm water to cover for 30 minutes, then drain. Cut off and discard stems; squeeze caps dry, thinly slice, and set aside.

Heat oil in a 10- to 12-inch frying pan over medium-high heat. Add garlic, ginger, and red pepper; stir once. Add turkey and cook, stirring, until meat is no longer pink (about 3 minutes); remove from pan and set aside.

Add bamboo shoots, water chestnuts, onions, and mushrooms to pan; cook, stirring, for 2 minutes. Return turkey to pan along with peas. Stir in Cooking Sauce; stir until sauce is thickened.

To serve, coat center of a lettuce leaf with hoisin sauce, if desired; spoon some of the turkey mixture on top, then roll up and eat out of hand. Makes 6 servings.

Cooking Sauce. Stir together 2 teaspoons **cornstarch**, 1 tablespoon **dry sherry**, 2 tablespoons *each* **reduced-sodium soy sauce** and **water,** and ½ teaspoon **sugar.**

Tomatillo Fish Stew

Per serving:

251 *calories* (29% fat, 25% carbohydrates, 46% protein),
8 g *total fat*, 1 g *saturated fat*, 36 mg *cholesterol*,
16 g *carbohydrates*, 29 g *protein*, 112 mg *sodium*

Preparation time: About 15 minutes

Cooking time: About 15 minutes

Here's a stew that can be ready to eat in minutes. Simply steep chunks of halibut in chicken broth flavored with white wine and tangy tomatillos.

- 1¼ **pounds tomatillos, husked**
- 1 **tablespoon olive oil**
- 1 **fresh jalapeño chile, thinly sliced**
- 1 **small onion, finely chopped**
- 1 **cup fresh or thawed frozen corn kernels**
- 3 **cups low-sodium chicken broth**
- ½ **cup slightly sweet white wine, such as Gewürztraminer or Chenin Blanc**
- 1 **pound halibut fillets or steaks, cut into 1-inch pieces**
- ½ **cup chopped parsley**

Thinly slice 3 of the tomatillos and set aside. Chop remaining tomatillos.

Heat oil in a 4- to 5-quart pan over medium-high heat. Add chopped tomatillos, chile, onion, and corn; cook, stirring occasionally, until mixture begins to brown (about 10 minutes). Add broth and wine; cover and bring to a boil. Stir in fish and sliced tomatillos. Remove from heat, cover, and let stand until fish is just slightly translucent or wet inside; cut in thickest part to test (about 1 minute). Stir in parsley just before serving. Makes 4 servings.

Veracruz Fish Salad

Per serving:

147 *calories* (19% fat, 21% carbohydrates, 60% protein),
3 g *total fat*, .5 g *saturated fat*, 83 mg *cholesterol*,
8 g *carbohydrates*, 22 g *protein*, 665 mg *sodium*

Preparation time: About 20 minutes, plus about 12 minutes to cook fish

Chilling time: At least 2 hours

Keep this chilled salad in mind for summer meals—it provides a welcome respite from hot entrées. Tomatoes, olives, and capers are tossed with lime juice and chunks of mahi mahi for a refreshing Latin-influenced meal.

- 2 **pounds mahi mahi or rockfish fillets**
- 4 **large tomatoes, coarsely diced**
- ⅔ **cup lime juice**
- 3 **cloves garlic, minced or pressed**
- 1 **cup sliced pimento-stuffed green olives**
- ⅓ **cup drained capers**
- ½ **cup thinly sliced green onions (including tops)**
  Salt and pepper
  About 12 large iceberg lettuce leaves
- 2 **limes, cut into wedges**

Rinse fish and pat dry. Place in a 9- by 13-inch baking dish, overlapping fillets slightly. Cover and bake in a 400° oven until just slightly translucent or wet inside; cut in thickest part to test (about 12 minutes). Let cool; then cover and refrigerate for at least 2 hours or up to 1 day.

Lift out fish; discard pan juices. Pull out and discard any bones. Break fish into bite-size chunks.

In a large bowl, combine fish, tomatoes, lime juice, garlic, olives, capers, and onions; mix gently. Season to taste with salt and pepper. Line a serving bowl with lettuce leaves; spoon in salad. Garnish with lime wedges. Makes 8 servings.

Seviche Salad

Per serving:
187 calories (8% fat, 46% carbohydrates, 46% protein),
2 g total fat, .3 g saturated fat, 54 mg cholesterol,
22 g carbohydrates, 23 g protein, 119 mg sodium

Preparation time: About 15 minutes

Chilling time: At least 3 hours

You don't need to turn on the heat to make this main-dish salad. Diced flounder tossed in a tangy lime marinade is served on crisp lettuce leaves and accompanied with slices of honeydew melon.

- 1 **small red onion**
- 1½ **pounds flounder fillets**
- ¾ **cup lime juice**
- ⅓ **cup fresh cilantro (coriander) leaves**
- 1 **medium-size honeydew melon (about 5 lbs.)**
  Romaine lettuce leaves

Cut 1 or 2 slices from onion, separate into rings, and refrigerate for garnish. Chop remaining onion; set aside.

Rinse fish, pat dry, and finely dice. Place in a large bowl and lightly mix in lime juice, chopped onion, and ¼ cup of the cilantro. Cover and refrigerate until fish is opaque (at least 3 hours) or for up to 1 day.

Quarter and seed melon. Cut each quarter lengthwise into ½-inch slices; remove rind. Spoon seviche into lettuce leaves; garnish with reserved onion rings and remaining cilantro. Arrange melon slices around seviche. Makes 6 servings.

Mussel & Potato Salad

Per serving:
189 calories (29% fat, 55% carbohydrates, 16% protein),
6 g total fat, .8 g saturated fat, 12 mg cholesterol,
26 g carbohydrates, 8 g protein, 218 mg sodium

Preparation time: About 25 minutes

Cooking time: About 30 minutes

Chilling time: At least 2 hours

Tender mussels and halved tiny potatoes tossed in a light, basil-accented vinaigrette make a hearty salad. If you like, prepare the salad the day before serving. Keep the skins on the potatoes for extra color.

- 1½ **pounds small red thin-skinned potatoes** (*each* 1½ **to 2 inches in diameter**)
  Basil Vinaigrette Dressing (recipe follows)
- 2 **pounds mussels in shells**
- 1 **jar (7 oz.) roasted red peppers, drained and cut into ¼-inch strips**
  Fresh basil sprigs

Place potatoes in a 3- to 4-quart pan; add enough water to cover. Bring to a boil over high heat; then reduce heat, cover, and boil gently until tender when pierced (about 20 minutes).

Meanwhile, prepare Basil Vinaigrette Dressing and set aside.

Drain potatoes; cut in half, place in a large bowl, and mix lightly with dressing. Let stand while cooking mussels.

Pull beards from mussels with a quick tug; scrub mussels and rinse well. Pour ¼ inch of water into a 5- to 6-quart pan. Add mussels, cover, and bring to a boil over high heat; reduce heat to low and cook until shells open (about 5 minutes). Discard any unopened mussels. When mussels are cool enough to handle, remove them from shells and add to potatoes; discard shells.

Add peppers to mussel-potato mixture; mix gently. Cover and refrigerate for at least 2 hours or up to 1 day. Spoon salad into a serving bowl and garnish with basil sprigs. Makes 6 servings.

Basil Vinaigrette Dressing. Combine ⅓ cup **seasoned rice vinegar** (or ⅓ cup white wine vinegar plus 1 teaspoon sugar), ⅓ cup finely chopped **fresh basil leaves,** 2 tablespoons **olive oil** or salad oil, 1 tablespoon **Dijon mustard,** ½ teaspoon **pepper,** and 1 clove **garlic,** minced or pressed. Mix until well blended.

Crab with Barbecue Sauce

Preparation time: About 5 minutes

Cooking time: About 1 hour

This is a messy meal —but a very tasty one! For the best flavor, use freshly cooked crab (if possible, have it killed, cooked, and cleaned while you wait).

- 2 **tablespoons margarine**
- 1 **medium-size onion, finely chopped**
- 3 **cloves garlic, minced or pressed**
- 1¾ **cups low-sodium chicken broth**
- 1 **can (8 oz.) no-salt-added tomato sauce**
- 1 **cup catsup**
- ½ **cup** *each* **white wine vinegar and firmly packed brown sugar**
- 3 **tablespoons Worcestershire**
- 1 **tablespoon reduced-sodium soy sauce**
- 1½ **teaspoons dry mustard**
- 1 **teaspoon** *each* **paprika and liquid hot pepper seasoning**

Per serving:
275 **calories** *(19% fat, 54% carbohydrates, 27% protein),*
6 g **total fat**, *.8 g* **saturated fat**, *54 mg* **cholesterol**,
38 g **carbohydrates**, *19 g* **protein**, *987 mg* **sodium**

- ½ **teaspoon** *each* **celery seeds, ground allspice, and dry thyme leaves**
- 2 **bay leaves**
- 3 **large cooked Dungeness crabs (5 to 6 lbs.** *total***), cleaned and cracked Sourdough bread, sliced (and toasted, if desired)**

Melt margarine in a 5- to 6-quart pan over medium heat. Add onion and garlic and cook, stirring occasionally, until onion is soft (about 10 minutes). Add broth, tomato sauce, catsup, vinegar, sugar, Worcestershire, soy, mustard, paprika, hot pepper seasoning, celery seeds, allspice, thyme, and bay leaves. Bring to a boil over high heat; reduce heat and simmer, uncovered, until reduced to 3 cups (about 45 minutes).

To serve sauce with cold crab, pour into individual bowls; dip crab into sauce. Or add crab to sauce and simmer until crab is heated through (about 5 minutes), stirring gently several times. Accompany crab and sauce with bread. Makes 6 servings.

Red Snapper & Shrimp

Preparation time: About 30 minutes

Cooking time: About 50 minutes

Two seafood lovers' favorites get together in this party dish. Snapper fillets topped with shrimp simmer to succulence in a chile-tomato sauce.

- 1 **tablespoon olive oil**
- 1 **medium-size onion, chopped**
- 1 **medium-size green bell pepper, seeded and chopped**
- 2 **cloves garlic, minced or pressed**
- 1 **small can (4 oz.) diced green chiles**
- 1 **large can (28 oz.) tomatoes, drained**
- ⅛ **teaspoon** *each* **salt and pepper**
- 1½ **pounds red snapper fillets, about ½ inch thick**
- ½ **pound medium-size raw shrimp (30 to 50 per lb.), shelled and deveined**
- 3 **tablespoons lemon juice**

Per serving:
156 **calories** *(21% fat, 18% carbohydrates, 61% protein),*
4 g **total fat**, *.6 g* **saturated fat**, *67 mg* **cholesterol**,
7 g **carbohydrates**, *23 g* **protein**, *374 mg* **sodium**

Heat oil in a 12- to 14-inch frying pan (preferably nonstick) over medium heat. Add onion, bell pepper, and garlic; cook, stirring occasionally, until onion is soft (about 10 minutes). Add chiles, tomatoes (break up with a spoon), salt, and pepper. Bring to a boil; reduce heat and simmer, uncovered, until sauce is thick (about 20 minutes).

Rinse fish fillets and pat dry. Arrange fillets in a single layer in sauce; distribute shrimp evenly over fish. Drizzle with lemon juice. Cover and simmer until shrimp are opaque throughout and fish is just slightly translucent or wet inside; cut in thickest part to test (about 15 minutes). Transfer fish and shrimp to a serving dish. Bring sauce to a boil; boil, stirring, until thickened (about 5 minutes). Pour sauce over fish and shrimp. Makes 8 servings.

This is truly a hands-on meal. Crab with Barbecue Sauce (recipe on facing page) is meant to be picked up and enjoyed along with two other finger foods, Quick Cuke Chips (recipe on page 13) and Jennie's Sweet & Sour Corn (recipe on page 32).

Kids' Sandwiches & Snacks

Anytime Granola

Children can enjoy this sweetened blend of oats, apricots, almonds, and wheat germ at any hour of the day. It can be topped with milk at breakfast, eaten plain as a midday snack, or sprinkled over yogurt for a light dinner (or a dessert).

- 8 cups old-fashioned rolled oats
- 1½ cups *each* firmly packed brown sugar and toasted wheat germ
- ½ cup *each* unsweetened shredded coconut and unsalted unroasted sunflower seeds
- 1 cup slivered blanched almonds
- 1½ cups golden raisins
- 2 cups chopped dried apricots
- 2 tablespoons grated orange peel
- ½ cup salad oil
- ¾ cup honey
- 2 teaspoons vanilla

In a large bowl, combine oats, sugar, wheat germ, coconut, sunflower seeds, almonds, raisins, apricots, and orange peel. Set aside. In a small pan, combine oil, honey, and vanilla. Cook over medium heat, stirring, until bubbly; pour over oat mixture and stir to mix well.

Grease 2 rimmed 10- by 15-inch baking pans; divide oat mixture evenly between pans. Bake, uncovered, in a 325° oven until lightly browned (about 25 minutes), stirring occasionally. Let cool in pans, stirring occasionally. Store airtight at cool room temperature for up to 1 month. Makes about 16 cups.

■

Per ¼ cup: 138 calories (28% fat, 63% carbohydrates, 9% protein), 4 g total fat, .7 g saturated fat, 0 mg cholesterol, 23 g carbohydrates, 3 g protein, 5 mg sodium

How do you change the diet of the adults in your family, yet still prepare food that pleases your children? It's quite a challenge—but the following snacks and sandwiches solve the problem to everybody's satisfaction. Research is continuing into the relationship between cholesterol levels in children and heart disease in adults. Most experts agree that attention to prudent eating patterns for children older than two who have elevated blood cholesterol could possibly help them have healthier futures. Let appealing recipes such as Meg's Micro Tacos and Anytime Granola introduce your kids to the pleasures of low-cholesterol, lowfat eating.

Homemade Peanut Butter & Banana Shake

Make your own peanut butter, then blend it with bananas, honey, yogurt, and milk for a perfect after-school pick-me-up.

- Homemade Peanut Butter (recipe follows)
- 2 medium-size ripe bananas
- ⅓ cup honey
- 2 cups *each* nonfat vanilla yogurt and nonfat milk

Prepare Homemade Peanut Butter. To peanut butter in food processor or blender, add bananas, honey, yogurt, and milk; whirl until smooth. Serve immediately. Makes about 5 cups (5 servings).

Homemade Peanut Butter. In a food processor or blender, combine ¾ cup **roasted unsalted peanuts** and 1½ teaspoons **salad oil;** whirl until smooth. Makes about ½ cup.

■

Per cup: 359 calories (30% fat, 56% carbohydrates, 14% protein), 13 g total fat, 2 g saturated fat, 5 mg cholesterol, 52 g carbohydrates, 14 g protein, 117 mg sodium

Pictured on page 31
Jennie's Sweet & Sour Corn

True finger food, these marinated corn-on-the-coblets are meant to be hand-held and nibbled. Make them one day and have them ready for snacking the next.

- 6 medium-size ears corn, cut into ¾-inch-thick rounds
- ¾ cup distilled white vinegar
- 1 cup minced onion
- 3 tablespoons sugar
- 1 jar (2 oz.) chopped pimentos, drained
- 1 teaspoon *each* mustard seeds and crushed red pepper
- ½ teaspoon salt

In a 6- to 8-quart pan, bring 4 quarts water to a boil over high heat. Add corn, cover, turn off heat, and let stand until corn kernels are tender (about 10 minutes). Drain and arrange in a 9- by 13-inch dish or on a rimmed platter.

In a small pan, combine vinegar, onion, sugar, pimentos, mustard seeds, red pepper, and salt. Bring to a boil; boil, stirring, until sugar is dissolved. Pour over corn; let cool, spooning marinade over corn frequently. Serve; or cover and refrigerate for up to 1 day (serve at room temperature). Drain corn before serving. Makes 12 servings.

■

Per serving: 60 calories (9% fat, 81% carbohydrates, 10% protein), .7 g total fat, .1 g saturated fat, 0 mg cholesterol, 14 g carbohydrates, 2 g protein, 100 mg sodium

Meg's Micro Tacos

Young cooks can prepare these bean- and cheese-topped flat tacos with very little help from adults. Because the tacos are microwaved, they can be ready to eat in minutes.

- 1 can (about 15 oz.) low-sodium kidney beans, drained and rinsed
- ¾ teaspoon chili powder
- 3 flour tortillas (*each* about 8 inches in diameter)
- ¾ cup *each* chopped lettuce and chopped tomato
- 3 tablespoons chopped onion
- 6 tablespoons shredded jack cheese

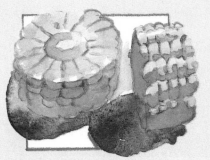

In a small bowl, mash beans with a potato masher; add chili powder. Set aside.

To make each taco, pierce a tortilla in several places with a fork. Brush lightly with water on both sides. Place tortilla between 2 paper towels and set on a dinner plate. Microwave on **HIGH (100%)** for 45 seconds to 1½ minutes or until tortilla is dry to the touch and almost crisp; do not overcook or tortilla may become too hard (it firms as it cools). Remove from oven and discard paper towels; wipe plate dry. Return tortilla to plate.

Spread ¼ cup of the mashed beans over tortilla to within ½ inch of edges. Top with ¼ cup each of the lettuce and tomato, then sprinkle with 1 tablespoon of the onion and 2 tablespoons of the cheese. Return to microwave; microwave, uncovered, on **HIGH (100%)** for 1 to 1½ minutes or until cheese is melted. Cut into wedges, if desired; serve immediately. Repeat with remaining tortillas. Makes 3 servings.

■

Per serving: 302 calories (16% fat, 64% carbohydrates, 20% protein), 5 g total fat, .1 g saturated fat, 12 mg cholesterol, 49 g carbohydrates, 15 g protein, 805 mg sodium

Oven-barbecued Burgers

Children will love these light-textured hamburgers coated with a sweet barbecue sauce.

- ½ cup nonfat milk
- 3 egg whites
- 1½ cups soft bread crumbs
- ½ teaspoon salt
- 1 teaspoon dry oregano leaves
- 1 large onion, cut into quarters
- 1½ pounds very lean ground beef
- 1 cup catsup
- 2 tablespoons *each* red wine vinegar, firmly packed brown sugar, and Worcestershire
- 1 tablespoon Dijon mustard
- 6 hamburger buns, preferably whole wheat, toasted

In a blender or food processor, combine milk, egg whites, bread crumbs, salt, oregano, and onion; whirl until puréed. In a large bowl, mix purée with beef. Form beef mixture into 6 patties, each about 3½ inches in diameter. Place patties in a 9- by 13-inch baking dish. Bake, uncovered, in a 375° oven for 25 minutes. Drain off fat.

Meanwhile, in a small pan, combine catsup, vinegar, sugar, Worcestershire, and mustard; bring to a boil over medium-high heat, stirring until sugar is dissolved. Spoon over beef patties. Bake for 10 more minutes. Serve on buns. Makes 6 servings.

■

Per serving: 502 calories (30% fat, 45% carbohydrates, 25% protein), 16 g total fat, 6 g saturated fat, 73 mg cholesterol, 56 g carbohydrates, 31 g protein, 1235 mg sodium

*Steamed Trout with Lettuce & Peas (recipe on facing page) arrives fresh
at your table with only a short stop in the steamer. Lemon peel, mint, and
garlic accent the vegetables that form a bed for rainbow trout.*

Fish & Clams in Black Bean Sauce

Per serving:
233 *calories* (30% fat, 9% carbohydrates, 61% protein),
8 g *total fat*, 1 g *saturated fat*, 65 mg *cholesterol*,
5 g *carbohydrates*, 34 g *protein*, 674 mg *sodium*

Preparation time: About 10 minutes

Cooking time: About 10 minutes

Mild, sweet rockfish and clams stand up well to a pungent black bean sauce. Since you steam this main course for two right on a heatproof serving dish, there's almost no clean-up after dinner.

- 1 pound rockfish fillets
- 1½ tablespoons fermented salted black beans, rinsed, drained, and patted dry
- 2 cloves garlic
- 1 tablespoon soy sauce
- 2 tablespoons dry sherry
- 3 green onions (including tops)
- 3 thin slices fresh ginger
- 12 small hard-shell clams, suitable for steaming, scrubbed
- 1 tablespoon salad oil

Rinse fish, pat dry, and place in a heatproof dish (about 1 inch deep) that is at least ½ inch smaller in diameter than your steamer.

In a small bowl, mince or mash black beans with garlic; stir in soy and sherry. Drizzle mixture over fish. Cut one of the onions into thirds; place cut onion and ginger on top of fish. Cut remaining 2 onions into 2-inch lengths, then cut lengths into thin shreds and set aside. Arrange clams around fish.

Pour about 1 inch of water into bottom of steamer; set rack in place. Cover steamer and bring water to a boil. Carefully place dish on rack. Cover and steam, keeping water at a steady boil, until fish is just slightly translucent or wet inside; cut in thickest part to test (about 5 minutes). If necessary, add boiling water to keep at least ½ inch of water in steamer. If fish is done before clams open, remove fish and continue to cook clams for a few more minutes until opened; then return fish to dish.

Using thick potholders, lift dish from steamer. Remove and discard ginger and onion pieces, then sprinkle onion slivers over fish. Heat oil in a small pan until it ripples when pan is tilted; pour over fish (oil will sizzle). Makes 2 servings.

Pictured on facing page

Steamed Trout with Lettuce & Peas

Per serving:
256 *calories* (20% fat, 22% carbohydrates, 58% protein),
6 g *total fat*, 1 g *saturated fat*, 88 mg *cholesterol*,
14 g *carbohydrates*, 37 g *protein*, 173 mg *sodium*

Preparation time: About 10 minutes

Cooking time: About 15 minutes

Steaming, a technique popular in Chinese cuisine, is a great way to cook without adding fat or losing flavor. Here, delicate trout steam with mint, peas, and lettuce for a pleasing light entrée.

- 3 tablespoons chopped fresh mint
- 1 tablespoon finely shredded lemon peel
- 1 clove garlic, minced or pressed
- 2 cups frozen tiny peas, thawed
- 3 cups shredded romaine lettuce
- 4 cleaned whole trout (about ½ lb. *each*)
- 8 to 12 lemon wedges

In a bowl, mix mint, lemon peel, garlic, peas, and lettuce. Pat mixture gently into a neat mound in a heatproof dish (about 1 inch deep) that is at least ½ inch smaller in diameter than your steamer. Arrange trout over pea mixture, cavity sides down and heads pointing in same direction; lean fish against each other. Arrange lemon wedges on top of fish.

Pour about 1 inch of water into bottom of steamer; set rack in place. Cover steamer and bring water to a boil. Carefully place dish on rack. Cover and steam, keeping water at a steady boil, until fish is just slightly translucent or wet inside; cut in thickest part to test (about 15 minutes). If necessary, add boiling water to keep at least ½ inch of water in steamer.

Using thick potholders, lift dish from steamer. Transfer trout to individual plates and spoon pea mixture alongside. Sprinkle trout with juice from lemon wedges. Makes 4 servings.

Dilled Fish in Parchment

Per serving:

270 *calories* (24% fat, 29% carbohydrates, 47% protein),
7 g *total fat*, 1 g *saturated fat*, 70 mg *cholesterol*,
19 g *carbohydrates*, 32 g *protein*, 123 mg *sodium*

Preparation time: About 25 minutes

Baking time: About 7 minutes

Cooking fish in parchment preserves every bit of flavor, keeps the fish juicy—and makes for a burst of delicious aroma when the packets are opened.

    1 tablespoon salad oil
    3 tablespoons *each* white wine vinegar and
       chopped green onions (including tops)
    1 teaspoon chopped fresh dill or ½ teaspoon
       dry dill weed
    1 teaspoon shredded tangerine or orange peel
    1 large can (1 lb.) mandarin oranges, drained
       Vegetable cooking spray
    4 sea bass fillets (6 oz. *each*), about 1 inch thick

In a small bowl, combine oil, vinegar, onions, dill, tangerine peel, and oranges; set aside.

Cut 4 pieces of parchment paper, each about 4 times wider and 6 inches longer than each fish fillet. Spray each sheet with cooking spray, starting 1 inch from the long side and covering an area the size of a fish fillet. Rinse fish and pat dry. Place one fillet on sprayed area of each sheet; spoon a fourth of the orange mixture over each.

Fold long edge of parchment closest to fish over fish; then roll over several times so fish is wrapped in parchment. With seam side down, double-fold each end of packet, pressing lightly to crease and tucking ends under packet.

Place packets, folded ends underneath, slightly apart in a baking pan; spray with cooking spray. Bake in a 500° oven until fish is just slightly translucent or wet inside (about 7 minutes); cut a tiny slit through parchment into fish to test. To serve, slash open packets and pull back parchment to reveal fish. Makes 4 servings.

Salmon with Vegetable Crest

Per serving:

407 *calories* (30% fat, 35% carbohydrates, 35% protein),
13 g *total fat*, 3 g *saturated fat*, 95 mg *cholesterol*,
35 g *carbohydrates*, 35 g *protein*, 287 mg *sodium*

Preparation time: About 10 minutes

Baking time: About 12 minutes

A creamy crown of vegetable-dotted Neufchâtel cheese tops salmon steaks in this one-dish dinner for two.

    2 medium-size thin-skinned potatoes
       (about 6 oz. *each*)
       Vegetable cooking spray
    2 salmon steaks (about 6 oz. *each*), about
       1 inch thick
    3 tablespoons lemon juice
    1 ounce Neufchâtel cheese, at room temperature
    ⅛ teaspoon *each* salt and pepper
    ¼ cup *each* grated carrot and chopped tomato
    2 tablespoons thinly sliced green onion
       (including top)
    1 tablespoon finely chopped parsley
       Lemon wedges

Cut potatoes into ¼-inch wedges. Spray a 9- by 13-inch baking pan with cooking spray. Rinse salmon and pat dry, then place salmon and potatoes in a single layer in pan; drizzle fish with 2 tablespoons of the lemon juice.

In a small bowl, mix cheese, salt, pepper, and remaining 1 tablespoon lemon juice until smooth and fluffy; lightly stir in carrot, tomato, onion, and parsley. Mound vegetable mixture evenly over fish, spreading nearly to edges.

Bake, uncovered, in a 400° oven until potatoes are tender and fish is just slightly translucent or wet inside; cut in thickest part to test (about 12 minutes). Serve with lemon wedges. Makes 2 servings.

Sole Florentine

Per serving:
115 **calories** (12% fat, 20% carbohydrates, 68% protein),
2 g **total fat**, .4 g **saturated fat**, 41 mg **cholesterol**,
6 g **carbohydrates**, 20 g **protein**, 192 mg **sodium**

Preparation time: About 25 minutes

Baking time: About 17 minutes

Spinach-filled rolls of delicate fish cook quickly in white wine; you can serve them in the baking dish.

- 6 **thin sole fillets (about 3 oz.** *each***)**
- 2 **pounds spinach, rinsed well, stems removed, and leaves coarsely chopped**
- ¼ **teaspoon ground nutmeg**
- 2 **tablespoons** *each* **grated lemon peel and chopped parsley**
- ¼ **cup** *each* **low-sodium chicken broth and dry white wine**
- 1 **small bay leaf**
- 4 **whole black peppercorns**

Rinse fish and pat dry. Trim each fillet into a rectangle measuring 3 by 8 inches (reserve trimmings); set aside. Finely chop trimmings; place in a bowl and combine with 1½ cups of the spinach, nutmeg, lemon peel, and parsley.

Spread spinach mixture over fillets. Gently roll up fillets, secure with wooden picks, and place in a 9-inch baking dish. Pour broth and wine around fish; add bay leaf and peppercorns. Cover and bake in a 400° oven for 10 minutes.

Place remaining spinach in another 9-inch baking dish. Lift fish rolls from first baking dish; arrange on top of spinach. Cover and bake until fish is just slightly translucent or wet inside; cut in thickest part to test (about 7 minutes). Makes 6 servings.

Broiled Fish Dijon

Per serving:
207 **calories** (29% fat, 9% carbohydrates, 62% protein),
7 g **total fat**, 2 g **saturated fat**, 59 mg **cholesterol**,
4 g **carbohydrates**, 31 g **protein**, 364 mg **sodium**

Preparation time: About 5 minutes

Cooking time: About 10 minutes

A bold blend of garlic and mustard complements the rich flavor of swordfish. Broiling makes the dish especially quick and easy.

- 6 **swordfish steaks (about ⅓ lb.** *each***), about 1 inch thick**
- 6 **small zucchini (about ¼ lb.** *each***), halved lengthwise**
- ¼ **cup lemon juice**
- 2 **tablespoons Dijon mustard**
- 1 **clove garlic, minced or pressed**
- ½ **teaspoon paprika**
- 2 **tablespoons drained capers**

Arrange fish and zucchini (cut sides up) in a single layer in a broiler pan. Drizzle with lemon juice.

In a small bowl, stir together mustard and garlic; spread over tops of steaks. Broil 6 to 8 inches below heat until zucchini is lightly browned and fish is just slightly translucent or wet inside; cut in thickest part to test (about 10 minutes). Rotate pan as necessary to cook fish evenly. Sprinkle fish and zucchini with paprika and capers. Makes 6 servings.

Oven-poached Lingcod

Per serving:

183 calories (20% fat, 18% carbohydrates, 62% protein), 4 g total fat, .6 g saturated fat, 79 mg cholesterol, 8 g carbohydrates, 28 g protein, 98 mg sodium

Preparation time: About 10 minutes

Cooking time: About 40 minutes

Poaching in white wine is the perfect way to cook mild lingcod. Mix a bit of the poaching liquid with sautéed leeks to make a memorable sauce.

- 2 medium-size onions, sliced
- 12 whole black peppercorns
- 4 whole allspice
- ⅓ cup lemon juice
- 2 bay leaves
- 1 cup dry white wine
- 8 cups water
- 2 pounds lingcod fillets, about 1 inch thick
- 3 large leeks (about 1 lb. *total*)
- 1 tablespoon olive oil
  Salt and pepper (optional)

In a 4- to 5-quart pan, combine onions, peppercorns, allspice, lemon juice, bay leaves, wine, and water. Bring to a boil; reduce heat, cover, and simmer for 20 minutes. Strain, then return liquid to pan.

Rinse fish, pat dry, and place in a single layer in a greased 9-inch baking dish. Bring strained poaching liquid to a boil; pour over fish (liquid should just cover fish; if necessary, add equal parts of hot water and wine to cover). Cover and bake in a 425° oven until fish is just slightly translucent or wet inside; cut in thickest part to test (about 6 minutes).

Lift fish from baking dish, drain well, place in a serving dish, and keep warm. Reserve ½ cup of the poaching liquid. Trim and discard all but about 3 inches of green tops from leeks; split leeks lengthwise, rinse well, and slice thinly. Heat oil in a 10- to 12-inch frying pan over medium heat; add leeks and cook, stirring occasionally, until soft (about 10 minutes). Add reserved ½ cup poaching liquid and bring to a boil; season to taste with salt and pepper, if desired. Pour sauce over fish. Makes 6 servings.

Pictured on facing page

Grilled Tuna with Teriyaki Fruit Sauce

Per serving:

361 calories (22% fat, 31% carbohydrates, 47% protein), 9 g total fat, 2 g saturated fat, 65 mg cholesterol, 28 g carbohydrates, 41 g protein, 673 mg sodium

Preparation time: About 15 minutes

Grilling time: About 3 minutes

Are tuna steaks best barbecued? You'll say yes when you taste this dish. The hot grilled steaks are served with papaya and a bold soy-ginger sauce.

- ¼ cup *each* sugar and reduced-sodium soy sauce
- 6 tablespoons sake or dry sherry
- 3 thin slices fresh ginger or ¼ teaspoon ground ginger
- 4 boneless and skinless tuna steaks (about 6 oz. *each*), about 1 inch thick
  Vegetable cooking spray
- 1 medium-size papaya (about 1 lb.), peeled, seeded, and cut into 12 wedges
- 2 teaspoons finely chopped candied or crystallized ginger
- 1 large green bell pepper, seeded and cut into thin slices

In a 2-quart pan, combine sugar, soy, sake, and ginger slices. Bring to a boil over high heat. Boil, stirring, until sugar is dissolved; then continue to boil until reduced to ⅓ cup. Discard ginger slices, if used. Keep warm.

Rinse fish and pat dry. Spray both sides of each steak with cooking spray. Place fish on a grill 4 to 6 inches above a solid bed of hot coals. Cook, turning once, until just slightly translucent or wet inside; cut in thickest part to test (about 3 minutes).

Place fish on a platter or individual plates. Evenly top with soy mixture, papaya, and candied ginger; arrange bell pepper alongside. Makes 4 servings.

Brighten up your next barbecue with Grilled Tuna with Teriyaki Fruit Sauce (recipe on facing page). Topped with a gingery sauce and served with thin slices of fresh papaya and bell pepper, the steaks can be prepared in next to no time.

Grilled Orange-Coriander Steak

Per serving:
190 calories (27% fat, 13% carbohydrates, 60% protein), 6 g total fat, 2 g saturated fat, 71 mg cholesterol, 6 g carbohydrates, 28 g protein, 53 mg sodium

Preparation time: About 10 minutes

Chilling time: At least 4 hours

Grilling time: About 8 minutes

Top round is at its juiciest best when soaked in a tangy orange marinade, then grilled just until rare. Thinly sliced and sauced with the marinade, it's sure to please the beef eaters in your family.

- 1 teaspoon grated orange peel
- ¾ cup orange juice
- 1 medium-size onion, minced
- 3 cloves garlic, minced or pressed
- ¼ cup white wine vinegar
- 1½ tablespoons ground coriander
- 1 teaspoon *each* cracked pepper and dry basil
- 1½ pounds lean top round steak, about 1 inch thick
  Finely shredded orange peel

In a bowl, stir together grated orange peel, orange juice, onion, garlic, vinegar, coriander, pepper, and basil. Measure out ½ cup of the mixture; cover and refrigerate until serving time.

Trim and discard any fat from steak; place steak in a shallow bowl. Pour remaining marinade over steak, cover, and refrigerate for at least 4 hours or until next day, turning steak over once or twice.

Remove steak from marinade and drain briefly, reserving marinade. Place steak on a lightly greased grill 4 to 6 inches above a solid bed of medium coals. Cook, turning once and basting often with marinade, until done to your liking; cut to test (about 8 minutes for rare). Meanwhile, heat reserved ½ cup marinade in a small pan over low heat.

To serve, cut steak across the grain into thin slices. Garnish with orange peel; accompany with heated marinade. Makes 6 servings.

Family Stew

Per serving:
497 calories (24% fat, 51% carbohydrates, 25% protein), 13 g total fat, 4 g saturated fat, 68 mg cholesterol, 65 g carbohydrates, 32 g protein, 603 mg sodium

Preparation time: About 15 minutes

Cooking time: About 2¾ hours

If you make this stew ahead, you'll reap a double reward: the flavor improves upon standing, and the fat solidifies, making it easy to remove.

- 1 tablespoon salad oil
- 1½ pounds top sirloin steak, cut into 1-inch cubes
- 2 large onions, chopped
- 2 cloves garlic, minced or pressed
- 2 cans (about 14 oz. *each*) tomatoes
- 1 can (14½ oz.) regular-strength beef broth
- ½ cup dry red wine
- ⅓ cup water
- 1 teaspoon *each* dry thyme leaves and dry marjoram leaves
- 6 large thin-skinned potatoes (about 3 lbs. *total*), unpeeled, cut into 1-inch cubes
- 2 cups 1-inch-long pieces celery
- 2 cups ½-inch-thick slices carrot
- ½ cup diced red bell pepper
- ¼ cup chopped parsley
- 1½ cups fresh or thawed frozen corn kernels

Heat oil in a 5- to 6-quart pan over medium-high heat. Add steak and cook, stirring as needed, until well browned on all sides (about 7 minutes). Add onions and garlic and cook, stirring occasionally, until onions are soft (about 7 minutes). Add tomatoes (break up with a spoon) and their liquid, broth, wine, water, thyme, and marjoram. Bring to a boil; then reduce heat, cover, and simmer until meat is very tender when pierced (about 2 hours).

Stir in potatoes, celery, carrot, and bell pepper. Cover and continue to simmer for 20 more minutes. Stir in parsley and corn; cover and continue to simmer until carrots are tender when pierced (about 5 more minutes). If made ahead, cover and refrigerate until next day. Lift off and discard fat; reheat stew, stirring often, over medium heat until hot (about 25 minutes). Makes 6 servings.

Fajitas Stir-fry

Per serving:
284 calories (29% fat, 27% carbohydrates, 44% protein), 9 g total fat, 2 g saturated fat, 66 mg cholesterol, 20 g carbohydrates, 32 g protein, 116 mg sodium

Preparation time: About 20 minutes

Cooking time: About 7 minutes

For traditional *fajitas,* strips of barbecued skirt steak are rolled in flour tortillas. This version is lower in fat: you stir-fry round steak and vegetables, then serve the mixture in crisp lettuce.

- 1 **pound lean top round steak**
- 1 **tablespoon salad oil**
- 2 **cloves garlic, minced or pressed**
- 1 **large onion, thinly sliced**
- 2 **fresh jalapeño chiles, seeded and minced**
- 1 **large red bell pepper, seeded and cut into thin strips**
- 2 **teaspoons ground cumin**
- 3 **tablespoons lime juice**
- 1 **teaspoon cornstarch**
- ½ **pound pear-shaped (Roma-type) tomatoes, diced**
- 1 **lime, cut into 8 wedges**
- 8 **large iceberg lettuce leaves, chilled**
- 1 **large onion, chopped**
- 1 **cup nonfat plain yogurt**

Cut steak with the grain into 1-inch-wide strips; then cut each strip across the grain into ⅛-inch-thick slices. Set aside. Heat oil in a wok or 12- to 14-inch frying pan over high heat; add meat and stir-fry until browned (1½ to 2 minutes). With a slotted spoon, transfer meat to a bowl.

Add garlic, sliced onion, chiles, and bell pepper to pan. Stir-fry until onion is soft (about 3 minutes). Stir together cumin, lime juice, and cornstarch; add to pan with meat and tomatoes. Stir until mixture comes to a boil, then transfer to a warm serving dish and garnish with lime wedges.

To eat, spoon meat mixture into lettuce leaves; add a squeeze of lime to taste and some of the chopped onion and yogurt. Fold up and eat out of hand. Makes 4 servings.

Szechwan Beef

Per serving:
300 calories (25% fat, 46% carbohydrates, 29% protein), 9 g total fat, 2 g saturated fat, 43 mg cholesterol, 38 g carbohydrates, 24 g protein, 392 mg sodium

Preparation time: About 15 minutes, plus 30 minutes to soak mushrooms

Cooking time: About 10 minutes

Carrot strips, cauliflowerets, and bamboo shoots add color and crispness to this beef stir-fry.

- **Cooking Sauce (recipe follows)**
- 8 **medium-size dried shiitake mushrooms (*each* about 2 inches in diameter)**
- 1 **pound lean top round steak**
- 1 **tablespoon salad oil**
- 16 **small dried hot red chiles**
- 1 **pound carrots, cut into thin 3-inch strips**
- 4 **cups bite-size pieces cauliflower**
- 2 **cans (about 8 oz. *each*) sliced bamboo shoots**
- 2 **cans (about 8 oz. *each*) sliced water chestnuts**

Prepare sauce; set aside. Soak mushrooms in warm water to cover for 30 minutes; drain. Cut off and discard stems; squeeze caps dry and thinly slice. Cut steak as for Fajitas Stir-fry (above).

Heat oil in a wok or 12- to 14-inch frying pan over medium-high heat. Add chiles and stir until chiles just begin to char. Remove chiles from pan.

Add meat to pan and stir-fry until browned (1½ to 2 minutes); remove with a slotted spoon and set aside. Add carrots, cauliflower, and mushrooms; stir-fry for 1 minute, then cover and cook until carrots and cauliflower are tender-crisp to bite (about 3 minutes). Drain bamboo shoots and water chestnuts, add to pan, and stir-fry for 1 more minute.

Return meat and chiles to pan; stir Cooking Sauce and add. Stir until sauce boils and thickens. Makes 6 servings.

Cooking Sauce. Mix 3 tablespoons **reduced-sodium soy sauce,** 1½ tablespoons **dry sherry,** 1 tablespoon **sugar,** and ¾ teaspoon **cornstarch.**

*Share this heart-shaped main course with someone you love. Mom's Magic
Meat Loaf (recipe on facing page) has a coating of tomato sauce and a lacy
trim of mashed potatoes. Garnish with a sprig of Italian parsley, if you like.*

Mom's Magic Meat Loaf

Per serving:
*487 **calories** (30% fat, 42% carbohydrates, 28% protein),*
*16 g **total fat**, 7 g **saturated fat**, 77 mg **cholesterol**,*
*50 g **carbohydrates**, 34 g **protein**, 661 mg **sodium***

Preparation time: About 30 minutes

Cooking time: About 1 hour

Who can resist a homey entrée like meat loaf? Add a touch of whimsy to this family favorite by shaping it in the form of a heart, covering it with bright red tomato sauce, and surrounding it with a fluffy border of mashed potatoes.

- **1 cup fine dry bread crumbs**
- **½ cup grated Parmesan cheese**
- **1 tablespoon dry basil**
- **½ teaspoon pepper**
- **4 egg whites**
- **2 cloves garlic, minced or pressed**
- **2 cans (8 oz. *each*) no-salt-added tomato sauce**
- **2 pounds ground lean top round**
- **3 pounds thin-skinned potatoes (*each* about 3 inches in diameter)**
- **1 large can (12 oz.) evaporated skim milk**
  Salt and pepper

In a large bowl, combine bread crumbs, cheese, basil, pepper, egg whites, garlic, and 1 cup of the tomato sauce. Add beef and mix lightly. In a rimmed shallow baking pan (about 10 inches in diameter), shape mixture into a 2-inch-thick heart. Bake in a 400° oven for 45 minutes. Remove from oven; carefully drain fat from pan, then top loaf with remaining tomato sauce. Bake for 15 more minutes.

While meat loaf is baking, place potatoes in a 3- to 4-quart pan and add water to cover. Bring to a boil over high heat; then reduce heat, cover, and boil gently until potatoes are tender when pierced (about 20 minutes). Drain and peel. Mash with a potato masher or electric mixer until smooth; slowly beat in milk. Season to taste with salt and pepper. Transfer meat loaf to serving plate. With a pastry bag fitted with a large star tip, pipe potatoes around meat loaf. (Or simply spoon potatoes around loaf.) Makes 8 servings.

Mustardy Veal Salad

Per serving:
*238 **calories** (17% fat, 49% carbohydrates, 34% protein),*
*5 g **total fat**, .9 g **saturated fat**, 72 mg **cholesterol**,*
*30 g **carbohydrates**, 21 g **protein**, 679 mg **sodium***

Preparation time: About 25 minutes

Cooking time: About 1¼ hours

First lightly sautéed, then oven-braised in a rich honey-mustard sauce, tender veal strips are served on a bed of chilled watercress sprigs and mandarin oranges for a special main-course salad.

- **Mustard Sauce (recipe follows)**
- **2 pounds boneless veal loin, trimmed of fat**
- **1 tablespoon salad oil**
- **2 large cans (1 lb. *each*) mandarin oranges, drained**
- **1 large red onion, thinly sliced**
- **2 pounds watercress sprigs**

Prepare Mustard Sauce; set aside.

Slice veal across the grain into ¼-inch strips. Heat oil in a 12- to 14-inch frying pan over medium-high heat. Add about half the veal; cook, stirring occasionally, until lightly browned (about 4 minutes). Remove veal from pan with a slotted spoon. Repeat with remaining veal.

In a shallow 2- to 2½-quart baking pan or casserole, mix meat with Mustard Sauce. Cover and bake in a 325° oven until meat is tender when pierced and sauce clings to meat (about 1 hour).

In a large bowl, toss mandarin oranges and onion with watercress. Top with hot veal. Makes 6 to 8 servings.

Mustard Sauce. In a small bowl, combine 1 small **onion,** chopped; ⅓ cup **Dijon mustard;** 3 tablespoons **honey;** 2 tablespoons **soy sauce;** 1 tablespoon **raspberry vinegar;** 1 tablespoon chopped **fresh rosemary** or 1½ teaspoons dry rosemary; 1 tablespoon finely chopped **fresh ginger;** and ¼ teaspoon coarsely ground **pepper.** Mix well.

Shepherd's Pie

Per serving:

*351 **calories** (21% fat, 45% carbohydrates, 34% protein), 8 g **total fat**, 3 g **saturated fat**, 82 mg **cholesterol**, 39 g **carbohydrates**, 30 g **protein**, 371 mg **sodium***

Preparation time: About 40 minutes

Baking & broiling time: About 20 minutes

The whole family will enjoy this hearty, savory pie. Beneath a creamy mashed-potato topping is a turkey and veal filling sweetly seasoned with cinnamon and cloves.

- 2 **pounds russet potatoes**
- 1 **cup evaporated skim milk**
- ½ **teaspoon ground white pepper**
- ¼ **teaspoon salt**
- 1 **pound ground veal**
- ½ **pound ground skinned turkey breast**
- 1 **large onion, chopped**
- 2 **cloves garlic, minced or pressed**
- 1½ **teaspoons** *each* **dry savory and dry thyme leaves**
- ½ **teaspoon dry mustard**
- ¼ **teaspoon ground cinnamon**
- ⅛ **teaspoon ground cloves**
- ½ **pound carrots, shredded**
- ½ **cup chopped parsley**
- 1 **cup regular-strength beef broth**

Place potatoes in a 3-quart pan and add water to cover. Bring to a boil over high heat; then reduce heat, cover, and boil gently until potatoes are tender when pierced (about 30 minutes). Drain; when cool enough to handle, peel and mash with milk, white pepper, and salt.

Meanwhile, crumble veal and turkey into a 12- to 14-inch frying pan. Cook over medium heat until opaque (about 10 minutes), stirring occasionally. With a slotted spoon, remove meat; drain off all but 1 tablespoon fat. Add onion and garlic to pan; cook over medium heat, stirring occasionally, until onion is soft (about 10 minutes). Add savory, thyme, mustard, cinnamon, and cloves and cook for 1 minute. Add carrots, parsley, broth, and meat; bring to a boil over high heat, then boil until liquid has evaporated (about 10 minutes). Transfer to a 2- to 3-quart casserole.

Spread mashed potatoes over meat mixture. Bake in a 375° oven until heated through (about 15 minutes), then broil 4 inches below heat until potatoes are lightly browned (about 5 minutes). Makes 6 servings.

Chayote with Spiced Lamb Filling

Per serving:

*192 **calories** (18% fat, 45% carbohydrates, 37% protein), 4 g **total fat**, 1 g **saturated fat**, 48 mg **cholesterol**, 23 g **carbohydrates**, 19 g **protein**, 279 mg **sodium***

Preparation time: About 1¼ hours

Baking time: About 25 minutes

For a change from the familiar, serve chayote filled with a simple ground lamb and onion stuffing.

- 3 **chayotes (about ¾ lb.** *each***)**
- 1 **pound ground lean lamb sirloin**
- 1 **medium-size onion, minced**
- 4 **cloves garlic, minced or pressed**
- ½ **teaspoon** *each* **ground allspice and coarsely ground pepper**
- ⅛ **teaspoon ground cloves**
- ⅓ **cup raisins**
- 1 **can (6 oz.) tomato paste**
- 2 **tablespoons dry red wine**

In a 4- to 5-quart pan, bring 8 cups water to a boil over high heat. Add chayotes; reduce heat, cover, and simmer until tender when pierced (about 40 minutes). Drain chayotes and let cool; halve lengthwise and scoop out pulp, leaving ½-inch-thick shells. Chop pulp. Invert shells to drain.

Crumble lamb into a 10- to 12-inch frying pan; add onion, garlic, allspice, pepper, and cloves. Cook over medium-high heat, stirring occasionally, until lamb is well browned (about 15 minutes). Stir in chayote pulp, raisins, tomato paste, and wine.

Spoon filling into chayote shells. Place in a 9- by 13-inch baking dish, cover, and bake in a 350° oven until filling is hot (about 25 minutes; uncover for last 5 minutes). Makes 6 servings.

Broiled Lamb Chops with Papaya Chutney

Per serving:
356 **calories** (24% fat, 52% carbohydrates, 24% protein),
10 g **total fat**, 3 g **saturated fat**, 57 mg **cholesterol**,
47 g **carbohydrates**, 22 g **protein**, 103 mg **sodium**

Preparation time: About 15 minutes

Cooking time: About 15 minutes

Broiled lamb chops are always a hit at dinnertime, especially when they're served juicy and still pink inside. Offer with homemade papaya chutney, chili-seasoned yogurt, and crisp raw cucumber for a complementary blend of flavors and textures.

    Seasoned Yogurt (recipe follows)
  8 single-rib lamb chops (about 1½ lbs. *total*), trimmed of fat
  ¼ cup *each* sugar and cider vinegar
  1 small onion, minced
  ½ cup raisins
  1 teaspoon *each* ground cinnamon and ground ginger
  1 large papaya (about 1¼ lbs.), peeled, seeded, and cut into ¼-inch-thick slices
  1 large cucumber (about ¾ lb.), seeded and cut into strips

Prepare Seasoned Yogurt; set aside.

Place lamb chops on a lightly greased rack in a broiler pan. Broil about 4 inches below heat, turning once, until well browned on both sides but still pink inside; cut to test (6 to 8 minutes).

Meanwhile, in a 10- to 12-inch frying pan, combine sugar, vinegar, onion, raisins, cinnamon, and ginger. Cook over medium-high heat, stirring occasionally, until onion is soft (about 7 minutes). Add papaya and stir gently until heated through (about 3 minutes). Place lamb chops on individual plates. Evenly top with papaya mixture. Serve Seasoned Yogurt and cucumber strips alongside. Makes 4 servings.

Seasoned Yogurt. In a small bowl, stir together 1 cup **nonfat plain yogurt**, 1 tablespoon **mustard seeds**, 1 teaspoon **sugar**, ¼ teaspoon **ground cumin,** and ⅛ teaspoon **chili powder** until well blended.

Japanese Country-style Pork & Potatoes

Per serving:
378 **calories** (29% fat, 42% carbohydrates, 29% protein),
11 g **total fat**, 3 g **saturated fat**, 76 mg **cholesterol**,
36 g **carbohydrates**, 26 g **protein**, 499 mg **sodium**

Preparation time: About 15 minutes

Cooking time: About 1¼ hours

Here's a stew with a difference: Japanese flavors. Soy, mirin, and sake season the pork and potatoes in this savory one-pot dinner.

  8 green onions (including tops)
  1 tablespoon salad oil
  1½ pounds lean boneless pork shoulder, trimmed of fat and cut into ½-inch cubes
  1 large onion, sliced
  ¼ cup reduced-sodium soy sauce
  ⅔ cup sake or dry vermouth
  ½ cup water
  ½ cup mirin (sweet rice wine) or cream sherry
  1½ pounds red thin-skinned potatoes, unpeeled, cut into ¼-inch-thick slices
  ¼ teaspoon pepper
  2 teaspoons sugar

Trim roots and any wilted ends from green onions. Then cut onions into 1-inch lengths, keeping green and white parts separate; set aside.

Heat oil in a 5- to 6-quart pan over medium-high heat. Add half the pork; cook, stirring, until well browned (about 10 minutes). Remove from pan and keep warm. Repeat with remaining pork.

Discard all but 1 tablespoon drippings from pan. Add sliced onion to pan and cook, stirring occasionally, until soft (about 7 minutes). Return pork to pan and add soy, sake, water, and mirin. Bring to a boil; then reduce heat, cover, and simmer for 25 minutes. Add potatoes, white part of green onions, pepper, and sugar. Return to a boil; then reduce heat, cover, and simmer until pork and potatoes are tender when pierced (about 25 minutes). Garnish with tops of green onions. Makes 6 servings.

Pork Medallions with Prunes

Per serving:
257 *calories* (23% fat, 38% carbohydrates, 39% protein),
6 g *total fat*, 1 g *saturated fat*, 74 mg *cholesterol*,
25 g *carbohydrates*, 25 g *protein*, 165 mg *sodium*

Preparation time: About 20 minutes

Cooking time: About 20 minutes

Tender pork and plump prunes are bathed in a rich Madeira sauce for an elegant entrée. For all its lavish looks and flavor, this dish is surprisingly quick and easy to make.

- 1 **pound pork tenderloin, trimmed of surface fat and cut across the grain into 1-inch-thick slices**
- ¾ **cup Madeira**
- ½ **cup regular-strength beef broth**
- 1 **tablespoon red wine vinegar**
- 2 **teaspoons cornstarch**
- 3 **whole cloves**
- 1 **tablespoon salad oil**
- ⅓ **cup chopped shallots**
- 12 **pitted prunes**
   Watercress sprigs

Place pork slices between sheets of plastic wrap or wax paper and gently pound with a flat-surfaced mallet to a thickness of ⅜ inch. Set aside.

In a small bowl, stir together Madeira, broth, vinegar, cornstarch, and cloves; set aside.

Heat oil in a 12- to 14-inch frying pan over medium-high heat. Add half the pork. Cook, turning once, until lightly browned on both sides and no longer pink in center; cut to test (about 5 minutes). Remove from pan, place in a serving dish, and keep warm; repeat with remaining pork.

Discard all but 1 tablespoon drippings from pan. Then add shallots to pan and cook, stirring occasionally, until soft (about 7 minutes). Add Madeira mixture. Cook, stirring occasionally, until sauce comes to a boil; remove cloves, then add prunes and heat through. Pour sauce and prunes over meat; garnish with watercress. Makes 4 servings.

Pictured on facing page

Green Chili with White Beans

Per serving:
441 *calories* (28% fat, 40% carbohydrates, 32% protein),
14 g *total fat*, 4 g *saturated fat*, 76 mg *cholesterol*,
44 g *carbohydrates*, 36 g *protein*, 1231 mg *sodium*

Preparation time: About 30 minutes

Cooking time: About 2 hours

Should chili be made with or without beans? Chili lovers may never stop arguing about that question—but this variation on the traditional dish could go a long way toward pleasing all those hungry for an answer.

- 3 **tablespoons salad oil**
- 2 **large green bell peppers, seeded and thinly sliced crosswise**
- 2 **cups sliced green onions (including tops)**
- 8 **cloves garlic, minced or pressed**
- 4 **teaspoons ground cumin**
- 6 **cans (13 oz. *each*) tomatillos**
- 4 **large cans (7 oz. *each*) diced green chiles**
- 6 **cans (15 oz. *each*) Italian white kidney beans (cannellini), drained; or 9 cups cooked small white beans, drained**
- 3 **pounds lean boneless pork shoulder or butt, trimmed of fat and cut into ½-inch cubes**
- 4 **teaspoons dry oregano leaves**
- ½ **teaspoon ground red pepper (cayenne)**
- ½ **cup lightly packed fresh cilantro (coriander) leaves**

Heat oil in a 10- to 12-quart pan over medium-high heat; add bell peppers, onions, garlic, and cumin. Cook, stirring, until onions are soft (about 5 minutes). Mix in tomatillos (break up with a spoon) and their liquid, chiles, beans, pork, oregano, and red pepper.

Bring to a boil; then reduce heat and simmer, stirring occasionally, until pork is tender when pierced (about 1¾ hours). For a thin chili, cook covered; for thicker chili, cook uncovered to desired consistency. Reserve a few cilantro leaves; chop remaining leaves. Stir chopped cilantro into chili; garnish with reserved leaves. Makes 12 servings.

Cozy up to a bowl of Green Chili with White Beans (recipe on facing page) and warm a winter evening. Lean pork, white beans, green chiles, and tomatillos simmer together for a hearty one-dish dinner. Be sure to save room for dessert: Fudgy Brownies (recipe on page 53) and Oatmeal Raisin Cookies (recipe on page 97).

Pasta, Grains & Legumes

Pasta is no stranger to the spotlight. Grains and legumes, though, are usually cast in supporting roles—and that's too bad, because these fiber-rich foods also deserve center stage. They're a good source of B vitamins and minerals; they're high in complex carbohydrates, providing energy without excess fat and calories.

Legumes and grains generally contain incomplete protein (lacking one or two essential amino acids), but you need only combine grains with legumes or add small amounts of meats, dairy products, or eggs to make the protein complete.

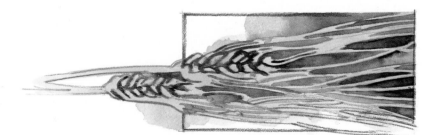

Fresh Vegetables with Fettuccine

Per serving:

320 **calories** *(12% fat, 73% carbohydrates, 15% protein),*
4 g **total fat**, *.9 g* **saturated fat**, *4 mg* **cholesterol**,
60 g **carbohydrates**, *13 g* **protein**, *122 mg* **sodium**

Preparation time: About 15 minutes

Cooking time: About 30 minutes

Appeal to the eye and the appetite with a rainbow of brightly colored vegetables served over broad strands of pasta.

- 1 tablespoon olive oil
- 1 large onion, chopped
- 3 cloves garlic, minced or pressed
- ¾ pound mushrooms, thinly sliced
- 3 pounds pear-shaped (Roma-type) tomatoes, thinly sliced
- 2 tablespoons chopped fresh basil leaves
- 1 pound dry eggless fettuccine or linguine
- ½ pound carrots, thinly sliced
- ¾ pound *each* crookneck squash and zucchini, thinly sliced
- ¼ cup *each* grated Parmesan cheese and thin strips of lean prosciutto

Heat oil in a 4- to 5-quart pan over medium-high heat. Add onion and cook, stirring occasionally, until soft (about 7 minutes). Add garlic and mushrooms; cook, stirring, until all liquid has evaporated (about 5 minutes). Add tomatoes and basil; continue to cook until mixture is thickened (about 10 more minutes), stirring occasionally.

Meanwhile, following package directions, cook fettuccine in boiling water until barely tender to bite; drain well. Place in a large, shallow serving bowl and keep warm.

Add carrots to sauce and cook for 5 minutes. Add crookneck squash and zucchini; continue to cook until vegetables are barely tender to bite (about 3 more minutes).

Spoon sauce over pasta and top with cheese and prosciutto. Makes 8 servings.

Spaghetti with Meat Sauce

Per serving:

349 **calories** *(28% fat, 48% carbohydrates, 24% protein),*
11 g **total fat**, *3 g* **saturated fat**, *51 mg* **cholesterol**,
43 g **carbohydrates**, *21 g* **protein**, *519 mg* **sodium**

Preparation time: About 10 minutes

Cooking time: About 30 minutes

Surprise! This familiar Italian-style meat sauce is made with ground turkey. For the lowest-fat sauce, use ground skinned turkey breast.

- 1 tablespoon olive oil
- 1 small onion, finely chopped
- ½ cup finely chopped green bell pepper
- ¼ pound carrots, finely shredded
- ⅓ cup thinly sliced mushrooms
- 1 tablespoon chopped parsley
- 1 clove garlic, minced or pressed
- 1 teaspoon dry basil
- ½ teaspoon *each* dry rosemary and dry oregano leaves
- 1 pound ground skinned turkey breast
- 1 large can (28 oz.) pear-shaped tomatoes
- 1 can (6 oz.) tomato paste
- ⅓ cup dry red wine
- 1 bay leaf
- 8 to 12 ounces dry spaghetti
  Grated Parmesan cheese (optional)

Heat oil in a 12- to 14-inch frying pan over medium-high heat. Add onion, bell pepper, carrots, mushrooms, parsley, garlic, basil, rosemary, and oregano; cook, stirring often, until onion is soft (about 5 minutes). Crumble turkey into pan and cook, stirring often, until lightly browned. Add tomatoes (break up with a spoon) and their liquid, tomato paste, wine, and bay leaf; bring to a boil. Adjust heat so sauce boils gently; cook, uncovered, stirring occasionally, until thickened (about 20 minutes). Discard bay leaf.

Meanwhile, following package directions, cook spaghetti in boiling water until barely tender to bite; drain well. Place in a large, shallow serving bowl. Pour sauce over noodles. Offer cheese, if desired, to add to taste. Makes 4 to 6 servings.

Let guests help themselves to a market basket of vegetables and cheese in our
Vegetable Lasagne (recipe on facing page). Carrots and zucchini alternate with
spinach and ricotta cheese, a mushroom-rich tomato sauce, mozzarella and
pasta. Round out a satisfying vegetarian meal with crusty bread and
quick-cooked green beans and crookneck squash.

Vegetable Lasagne

Per serving:
602 *calories* (30% fat, 44% carbohydrates, 26% protein),
21 g *total fat*, 8 g *saturated fat*, 36 mg *cholesterol*,
70 g *carbohydrates*, 41 g *protein*, 654 mg *sodium*

Preparation time: About 30 minutes

Cooking time: About 45 minutes

Looking for a meatless main dish? Try this lasagne. Pasta, vegetables, and cheeses are layered with an herbed tomato sauce enriched with tofu.

- 1 **pound firm tofu**
- 1 **package (8 oz.) dry lasagne noodles**
- 1 **pound carrots, cut into ¼-inch-thick slices**
- 1 **pound zucchini, cut into ¼-inch-thick slices**
- 1 **tablespoon olive oil or salad oil**
- 1 **large onion, chopped**
- 1 **pound mushrooms, thinly sliced**
- 1 **teaspoon** *each* **dry basil, dry thyme leaves, and dry oregano leaves**
- 2 **large cans (15 oz.** *each***) no-salt-added tomato sauce**
- 1 **can (6 oz.) tomato paste**
- 2 **packages (10 oz.** *each***) frozen chopped spinach, thawed and squeezed dry**
- 1 **cup (about 8 oz.) part-skim ricotta cheese**
- 2 **cups (8 oz.) shredded skim mozzarella cheese**
- ¼ **cup grated Parmesan cheese**

Break tofu into coarse chunks and drain in a colander. With paper towels, press tofu to remove excess liquid. Set aside.

In a 5- to 6-quart pan, bring 3 quarts water to a boil over high heat. Add noodles and carrots; cook for 6 minutes. Add zucchini; continue to cook until noodles are just tender to bite (about 4 more minutes). Drain well; set vegetables and noodles aside separately.

Heat oil in same pan over medium-high heat. Add tofu, onion, mushrooms, basil, thyme, and oregano. Cook, stirring often, until onion is soft and liquid has evaporated (about 7 minutes). Add tomato sauce and tomato paste; stir to blend, then set aside. Mix spinach and ricotta cheese; set aside.

Spread a third of the sauce in a 9- by 13-inch baking dish. Arrange half the noodles over sauce; sprinkle evenly with half *each* of the carrots, zucchini, spinach mixture, and mozzarella cheese. Repeat layers; then spread remaining sauce on top. Sprinkle with Parmesan cheese.

Set baking dish in a rimmed baking pan to catch any drips. Bake, uncovered, in a 400° oven until hot in center (about 25 minutes). Let stand for 5 minutes before serving. Makes 6 servings.

Korean Noodles with Hot Sauce

Per serving:
265 *calories* (16% fat, 71% carbohydrates, 13% protein),
5 g *total fat*, .5 g *saturated fat*, 0 mg *cholesterol*,
47 g *carbohydrates*, 9 g *protein*, 367 mg *sodium*

Preparation time: About 10 minutes

Cooking time: About 8 minutes

The ingredients for this simple entrée are sold in most well-stocked supermarkets. Cucumber slices offer a welcome cool contrast to the spicy sauce.

- 1 **tablespoon Oriental sesame oil**
- 3 **tablespoons distilled white vinegar**
- 1 to 2 **tablespoons hot bean paste**
- 2 **tablespoons soy sauce**
- 3 **tablespoons sliced green onions (including tops)**
- 1 **clove garlic, minced**
- 1 **teaspoon** *each* **sugar and pepper**
- 2 **teaspoons minced fresh ginger**
- 2 **tablespoons sesame seeds**
- 12 **ounces dry buckwheat noodles**
- 1 **medium-size cucumber, thinly sliced**

In a bowl, combine sesame oil, vinegar, bean paste, soy, onions, garlic, sugar, pepper, and ginger. Set aside. Toast sesame seeds in a small frying pan over medium heat until golden (about 3 minutes), shaking pan frequently. Set aside.

Following package directions, cook noodles in boiling water until barely tender to bite. Drain; return to pan and add vinegar mixture and sesame seeds. Mix well. Garnish with cucumber. Makes 4 to 6 servings.

Recipe Makeovers

Fried Chicken

When you're changing your eating habits, one of the greatest challenges is giving up tried-and-true dishes that don't meet the requirements of your new diet. Still, there's a way to adhere to your revised eating pattern and enjoy old favorites: adapt them to fit the new guidelines. By changing cooking techniques and using ingredients lower in cholesterol and fat, you can make quite a difference in a recipe's nutritional value—without drastically affecting its taste, texture, and appearance.

On this page, you can see how we revised two favorites: fried chicken and brownies.

Using these examples as models, you can start converting your own favorite recipes. With our recommended cooking methods, the help of the herb and spice list on page 107 and the substitution list on page 108, and a little experimentation, you'll create some healthful new traditions.

In converting Easy Fried Chicken to Easy Oven-fried Chicken, we cut fat from 55% to 15% of total calories by baking skinned chicken breasts rather than shallow-frying a whole cut-up chicken. Cholesterol was cut in half; total calories dropped by two-thirds. For extra fiber and texture, we substituted whole wheat bread crumbs and cornmeal for flour; the flavor gets a boost from fresh garlic and additional spices.

■ Before
Easy Fried Chicken

1 frying chicken (about 3 lbs.), cut up
2 tablespoons dry sherry
½ cup all-purpose flour
1 teaspoon *each* salt and garlic salt
½ teaspoon paprika
¼ teaspoon *each* pepper, dry sage leaves, dry thyme leaves, and dry basil
About 2½ cups salad oil

Place chicken in a shallow baking pan and sprinkle with sherry; let stand for 10 minutes. Meanwhile, in a plastic bag, combine flour, salt, garlic salt, paprika, pepper, sage, thyme, and basil. Pour ½ inch of oil into a wide, heavy frying pan with a lid. Lift chicken from baking pan; do not pat dry. Place chicken, a few pieces at a time, in bag and shake to coat. Arrange chicken, skin side down, in unheated oil; do not crowd pan.

Cover pan and place over medium-high heat. When chicken begins sizzling loudly (after about 7 minutes), begin timing; cook for 15 minutes. Turn pieces over with tongs and continue to cook, uncovered, until meat near thighbone is no longer pink; cut to test (about 10 more minutes). Lift out chicken and drain briefly on paper towels. Serve hot or let cool to room temperature. Makes 4 servings.

Per serving: 511 calories (55% fat, 11% carbohydrates, 34% protein), 31 g total fat, 7 g saturated fat, 132 mg cholesterol, 13 g carbohydrates, 43 g protein, 627 mg sodium

■ After
Easy Oven-fried Chicken

2 tablespoons dry sherry
2 cloves garlic, minced or pressed
2 whole chicken breasts, skinned, boned, and split (about 1 lb. meat total)
½ cup soft whole wheat bread crumbs
2 tablespoons cornmeal
½ teaspoon salt
1 teaspoon paprika
½ teaspoon *each* pepper, dry sage leaves, dry thyme leaves, and dry basil
1 teaspoon salad oil

In a shallow bowl, combine sherry and garlic. Add chicken, turn to coat, and let stand for about 20 minutes.

In another shallow bowl, combine bread crumbs, cornmeal, salt, paprika, pepper, sage, thyme, and basil. Dip each chicken piece in crumb mixture to coat.

Brush a rimmed 10- by 15-inch baking pan with oil. Arrange chicken, skinned side up, in pan. Bake, uncovered, in a 450° oven until meat is no longer pink in thickest part; cut to test (about 20 minutes). Serve hot or let cool to room temperature. Makes 4 servings.

Per serving: 175 calories (15% fat, 20% carbohydrates, 65% protein), 3 g total fat, .6 g saturated fat, 66 mg cholesterol, 8 g carbohydrates, 27 g protein, 382 mg sodium

Brownies

Replacing butter with margarine makes our Fudgy Brownies lower in cholesterol than the original Fudge Brownies. To reduce fat, we used cocoa instead of chocolate and decreased the quantity of walnuts, sprinkling the nuts on top of the batter (rather than mixing them into it) to play up their flavor and crisp texture. Substituting egg whites for whole eggs eliminates both fat and cholesterol. Total calories were reduced by about a third, with fat calories dropping from 50% to 29% of the total. Cholesterol was cut by more than three-fourths—without any loss in taste.

■ Before
Fudge Brownies

- 10 tablespoons butter
- 4 ounces unsweetened chocolate
- 2 cups sugar
- 1½ teaspoons vanilla
- 4 eggs
- 1 cup all-purpose flour
- 1 cup coarsely chopped walnuts

In a 2- to 3-quart pan, melt butter and chocolate over medium-low heat, stirring until well blended. Remove from heat and stir in sugar and vanilla. Add eggs, one at a time, beating well after each addition. Stir in flour; then mix in walnuts.

Spread batter evenly in a greased 9-inch square baking pan. Bake in a 325° oven until brownies feel dry on top (about 35 minutes). Let cool in pan on a rack, then cut into 2¼-inch squares. Store airtight. Makes 16 brownies.

Per brownie: 293 calories (50% fat, 45% carbohydrates, 5% protein), 17 g total fat, 7 g saturated fat, 88 mg cholesterol, 35 g carbohydrates, 4 g protein, 92 mg sodium

■ After
Fudgy Brownies

- 7 tablespoons margarine
- ¾ cup unsweetened cocoa
- 2 cups sugar
- 1½ teaspoons vanilla
- 1 egg
- 5 egg whites
- 1 cup all-purpose flour
- 2 tablespoons finely chopped walnuts

In a 2- to 3-quart pan, combine margarine and cocoa; stir over medium-low heat until margarine is melted and mixture is well blended. Remove from heat and stir in sugar and vanilla. Mix in egg and egg whites until blended. Stir in flour.

Spread batter evenly in a greased 9-inch square baking pan. Sprinkle walnuts over batter. Bake in a 325° oven until brownies feel dry on top (about 35 minutes). Let cool in pan on a rack, then cut into 2¼-inch squares. Store airtight. Makes 16 brownies.

Per brownie: 197 calories (29% fat, 65% carbohydrates, 6% protein), 7 g total fat, 1 g saturated fat, 17 mg cholesterol, 33 g carbohydrates, 3 g protein, 79 mg sodium

Noodles with Pork & Peanut Sauce

Per serving:
367 **calories** (26% fat, 48% carbohydrates, 26% protein), 11 g **total fat**, 3 g **saturated fat**, 51 mg **cholesterol**, 44 g **carbohydrates**, 24 g **protein**, 656 mg **sodium**

Preparation time: About 10 minutes

Cooking time: About 10 minutes

Putting this stir-fry on the table takes less than half an hour. Just brown a pound of lean pork, mix with nippy mustard greens and a creamy peanut sauce, and serve over fine noodles.

  Peanut Sauce (recipe follows)
1 **pound ground lean pork**
4 **cloves garlic, minced or pressed**
1 **large onion, cut lengthwise into slender strips**
10 **ounces dry capellini**
1½ **cups lightly packed slivered mustard greens**

Prepare Peanut Sauce and set aside.

Crumble pork into a 10- to 12-inch frying pan; add garlic and onion. Cook over medium-high heat, stirring, until pork is well browned (about 7 minutes). Drain well and return to pan.

While pork is cooking, following package directions, cook capellini in boiling water until barely tender to bite; drain well. Place in a large, shallow serving bowl and keep warm.

To browned pork, add Peanut Sauce and 1 cup of the mustard greens; bring to a boil, stirring. Stir pork mixture into drained noodles; top with remaining ½ cup mustard greens. Makes 6 servings.

Peanut Sauce. Stir together ¼ cup *each* **reduced-sodium soy sauce** and **low-sodium chicken broth**, 2 tablespoons *each* **creamy peanut butter** and **hoisin sauce**, and 2 teaspoons **sugar.**

Pictured on facing page

Basil & Scallop Pasta Salad

Per serving:
336 **calories** (28% fat, 47% carbohydrates, 25% protein), 11 g **total fat**, 1 g **saturated fat**, 25 mg **cholesterol**, 40 g **carbohydrates**, 22 g **protein**, 150 mg **sodium**

Preparation time: About 20 minutes

Cooking time: About 15 minutes

Chilling time: At least 2 hours

Make this cold salad ahead to enjoy on a hot summer evening. Small pasta seashells are an eye-catching complement to the tender fresh scallops.

8 **ounces dry seashell-shaped pasta**
1 **pound sea scallops**
4 **cups broccoli flowerets, cut into bite-size pieces**
¼ **cup** *each* **lemon juice, white wine vinegar, and olive oil**
1 **teaspoon** *each* **dry mustard and sugar**
1 **clove garlic, minced or pressed**
1 **cup finely chopped fresh basil leaves**
  Small inner leaves from 2 large heads romaine lettuce (about 30 leaves)
  Lemon wedges

Following package directions, cook pasta in boiling water until barely tender to bite. Drain, rinse with cold water, and drain again.

If scallops are thicker than ¼ inch, cut them in half horizontally. Set scallops aside. In a 12- to 14-inch frying pan, bring ¼ inch water to a boil over high heat. Add broccoli, cover, and cook just until tender-crisp to bite (about 4 minutes); drain and immerse in cold water to cool. Meanwhile, in same pan, bring another ¼ inch water to a gentle boil over medium-high heat. Add scallops, cover, and cook just until opaque throughout; cut to test (about 3 minutes). Drain both broccoli and scallops; set aside.

In a large bowl, combine lemon juice, vinegar, oil, mustard, sugar, garlic, and basil; mix well. Add pasta, broccoli, and scallops; mix gently. Cover and refrigerate for at least 2 hours or up to 1 day. Divide romaine leaves equally among 6 individual plates; top with scallop mixture. Garnish with lemon wedges, if desired. Makes 6 servings.

Cool off at dinner with this make-ahead meal. Served on crisp lettuce and
garnished with lemon wedges, Basil & Scallop Pasta Salad (recipe on facing
page) combines seafood and pasta seashells in a refreshing lemon vinaigrette.

Oriental Pasta Primavera

Per serving:
*304 **calories** (11% fat, 70% carbohydrates, 19% protein),*
*4 g **total fat**, .4 g **saturated fat**, 0 mg **cholesterol**,*
*55 g **carbohydrates**, 14 g **protein**, 186 mg **sodium***

Preparation time: About 20 minutes, plus 30 minutes to soak mushrooms

Cooking time: About 20 minutes

This Asian-accented dish of pasta and vegetables is every bit as satisfying as the Italian original.

- 2 **tablespoons sesame seeds**
- 8 **large dried or fresh shiitake mushrooms (***each* **about 3 inches in diameter)**
- ½ **pound** *each* **asparagus and bok choy**
- 1 **can (15 oz.) miniature corn, drained**
- 1 **pound dry whole wheat spaghetti**
- 1 **tablespoon salad oil**
- 2 **cloves garlic, minced or pressed**
- 1 **tablespoon very finely chopped fresh ginger**
- ½ **pound Chinese pea pods (also called snow or sugar peas) or sugar snap peas, ends and strings removed**
- 1 **can (about 8 oz.) sliced water chestnuts, drained**
- ¼ **cup dry sherry**
- 1 **cup low-sodium chicken broth**
- 2 **tablespoons reduced-sodium soy sauce**
- 1 **teaspoon** *each* **sugar and white wine vinegar**

Toast sesame seeds in a small frying pan over medium heat until golden (about 3 minutes), shaking pan frequently. Pour out of pan and set aside.

If using dried mushrooms, soak in warm water to cover for 30 minutes, then drain. Cut off and discard stems; squeeze caps dry and thinly slice. Or trim any tough stems from fresh mushrooms; thinly slice caps.

Snap off and discard tough ends of asparagus. Cut asparagus spears, bok choy stems and leaves, and corn into ½-inch slanting slices. Set aside.

Following package directions, cook spaghetti in boiling water until barely tender to bite; drain well. Place in a large, shallow serving bowl and keep warm.

Heat oil in a 12- to 14-inch frying pan over high heat. Add garlic and ginger and cook, stirring, until lightly browned (about 30 seconds). Add mushrooms, asparagus, bok choy, corn, pea pods, water chestnuts, and sherry. Cover and cook, stirring often, until vegetables are tender-crisp to bite (about 2 minutes). Spoon vegetables over noodles.

Add broth, soy, sugar, and vinegar to wok; bring to a boil, stirring. Pour over noodles and vegetables. Sprinkle with sesame seeds, then mix lightly. Serve immediately. Makes 8 servings.

Green Pasta with Spinach Pesto

Per serving:
*314 **calories** (23% fat, 58% carbohydrates, 19% protein),*
*8 g **total fat**, 3 g **saturated fat**, 59 mg **cholesterol**,*
*46 g **carbohydrates**, 15 g **protein**, 205 mg **sodium***

Preparation time: About 10 minutes

Cooking time: About 10 minutes

For a twist on tradition, make pesto sauce with spinach instead of basil, and use a cupful of tart yogurt in place of most of the oil.

- 1 **pound spinach, rinsed well, stems removed** **Spinach Pesto (recipe follows)**
- 1 **pound dry spinach noodles**
- ½ **cup minced red onion**
- 1 **cup radishes, thinly sliced**

Cut spinach leaves into thin shreds. Measure out 1 cup, lightly packed, for pesto; set remaining shredded leaves aside.

Prepare pesto. Following package directions, cook noodles in boiling water until barely tender to bite; drain well. Place in a large, shallow serving bowl. Pour pesto on noodles; sprinkle with remaining shredded spinach, onion, and radishes. Toss with 2 forks to mix. Makes 6 to 8 servings.

Spinach Pesto. In a blender or food processor, combine the 1 cup **reserved shredded spinach**, 1 clove **garlic**, 2 tablespoons **pine nuts**, ½ cup grated **Parmesan cheese**, 1 cup **nonfat plain yogurt**, and 1 tablespoon **olive oil**. Whirl until puréed.

Vegetable & Bulgur Stir-fry

Per serving:

329 **calories** (26% fat, 59% carbohydrates, 15% protein), 10 g **total fat**, .6 g **saturated fat**, 12 mg **cholesterol**, 51 g **carbohydrates**, 12 g **protein**, 118 mg **sodium**

Preparation time: About 15 minutes

Cooking time: About 20 minutes

A market basket of bright vegetables joins nutty-tasting bulgur in this quick stir-fry. It's an attractive and satisfying main dish for four.

> 1 tablespoon salad oil
> 1 cup bulgur
> 1 tablespoon sesame seeds
> 1 clove garlic, minced or pressed
> ½ cup sliced green onions (including tops)
> ½ pound carrots, thinly sliced
> ½ pound *each* zucchini and crookneck squash, thinly sliced
> ¼ pound mushrooms, thinly sliced
> ½ teaspoon *each* dry basil, dry marjoram leaves, and dry oregano leaves
> ⅛ teaspoon pepper
> 1¾ cups water
> 2 cups broccoli flowerets
> ½ cup shredded jack cheese
>   Lemon wedges

Heat oil in a 12- to 14-inch frying pan (preferably nonstick) over medium-high heat. Add bulgur, sesame seeds, garlic, and onions; cook, stirring, for 2 minutes. Add carrots and cook, stirring, for 2 minutes. Add zucchini, crookneck squash, and mushrooms and continue to cook for 1 more minute.

Add basil, marjoram, oregano, pepper, and water; reduce heat, cover, and simmer for 5 minutes. Add broccoli and cook until liquid is absorbed (about 5 more minutes). Sprinkle with cheese. Serve with lemon wedges. Makes 4 servings.

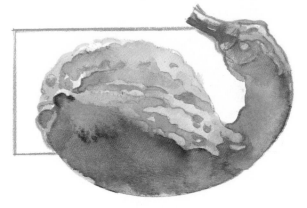

Bulgur & Rice Pilaf

Per serving:

140 **calories** (20% fat, 71% carbohydrates, 9% protein), 3 g **total fat**, .3 g **saturated fat**, 0 mg **cholesterol**, 25 g **carbohydrates**, 3 g **protein**, 365 mg **sodium**

Preparation time: About 10 minutes, plus 1 hour to soak bulgur

Cooking time: About 1¼ hours

Even the youngest members of the family will enjoy this mild two-grain pilaf. It's delicious with baked or broiled chicken.

> 2 cups regular-strength chicken broth
> ½ cup bulgur
> 1 tablespoon margarine
> 1 small onion, finely chopped
> 1 stalk celery, finely chopped
> ¼ cup lightly packed chopped celery leaves
> ¼ teaspoon pepper
> ½ cup brown rice
> 1 large bay leaf
>   Whole celery leaves

In a 1- to 2-quart pan, bring 1 cup of the broth to a boil. Remove from heat; add bulgur. Cover and set aside until broth is absorbed (about 1 hour).

Meanwhile, melt margarine in a 3- to 4-quart pan over medium-high heat. Add onion, celery, chopped celery leaves, and pepper; cook, stirring, until onion is soft but not browned (about 5 minutes). Add rice and cook, stirring, until opaque (about 3 more minutes). Mix in bay leaf and remaining 1 cup broth. Increase heat to high and bring mixture to a boil; reduce heat, cover, and simmer until all liquid is absorbed (about 1 hour).

Lightly mix bulgur into rice mixture and transfer to a warm serving dish. Garnish with whole celery leaves. Makes 6 servings.

Red bell peppers and fresh Anaheim and jalapeño chiles are mixed with grain from the Middle East in Couscous & Chiles (recipe on facing page). Accented with olives, raisins, and cool yogurt, it's a filling entrée. To complete the meal, just add your favorite fresh fruit.

Pictured on facing page

Couscous & Chiles

Per serving:
*166 calories (15% fat, 71% carbohydrates, 14% protein),
3 g total fat, .4 g saturated fat, .5 mg cholesterol,
30 g carbohydrates, 6 g protein, 81 mg sodium*

Preparation time: About 10 minutes

Cooking time: About 30 minutes

Here's a multinational dish! Couscous, raisins, and olives, all typical of the Middle East, join up with familiar Latin American ingredients—chiles, cumin, and fresh lime juice.

- 1 **tablespoon olive oil**
- 1 **medium-size onion, chopped**
- 1 **large clove garlic, minced or pressed**
- 1 **large red bell pepper, seeded and chopped**
- 1 **medium-size fresh Anaheim (California) chile, seeded and chopped**
- 1 **fresh jalapeño chile, seeded and finely chopped**
- 1 **tablespoon *each* ground cumin and chili powder**
- 2 **cups low-sodium chicken broth**
- 2 **tablespoons lime juice**
- 2 **cups couscous**
- ¼ **cup golden raisins**
- ½ **cup frozen tiny peas, thawed**
- 1 **large firm-ripe tomato, peeled, seeded, and chopped**
- ¼ **cup sliced ripe olives**
  Fresh cilantro (coriander) sprigs
- 1 **cup nonfat plain yogurt**

Heat oil in a 5- to 6-quart pan over medium heat. Add onion, garlic, bell pepper, Anaheim chile, and jalapeño chile. Cook, stirring occasionally, until onion is golden (about 15 minutes). Stir in cumin, chili powder, broth, and lime juice. Bring to a boil over high heat. Add couscous and raisins; stir well. Cover, remove from heat, and let stand until liquid is absorbed (about 5 minutes). Mix in peas, tomato, and olives. Cover and let stand until flavors are blended (about 3 minutes).

Spoon couscous onto a platter or individual plates. Garnish each serving with cilantro and a spoonful of yogurt. Makes 8 to 10 servings.

Ratatouille Rice

Per serving:
*187 calories (14% fat, 76% carbohydrates, 10% protein),
3 g total fat, .2 g saturated fat, 0 mg cholesterol,
37 g carbohydrates, 5 g protein, 454 mg sodium*

Preparation time: About 10 minutes

Cooking time: About 1¼ hours

The popular French "stew" of bell peppers, tomatoes, and eggplant shows up in a new guise—mixed with rice and baked in a casserole.

- 1 **tablespoon olive oil**
- 1 **medium-size onion, chopped**
- 3 **cloves garlic, minced or pressed**
- ½ **pound mushrooms, sliced**
- 1 **large green bell pepper, seeded and chopped**
- 1 **small eggplant (about ¾ lb.), unpeeled, cut into ½-inch cubes**
- 1 **large can (15 oz.) tomato sauce**
- 1 **cup regular-strength chicken broth**
- 1½ **teaspoons dry thyme leaves**
- 1½ **cups brown rice**

Heat oil in a 10- to 12-inch frying pan (preferably nonstick) over medium-high heat. Add onion and cook, stirring occasionally, until soft (about 7 minutes). Add garlic and cook for 1 minute. Add mushrooms, bell pepper, and eggplant; cook, stirring, until liquid has evaporated (about 5 minutes).

In a 3- to 4-quart casserole or baking dish, combine eggplant mixture with tomato sauce, broth, thyme, and rice. Cover and bake in a 350° oven until rice is tender to bite (about 1 hour). Makes 6 to 8 servings.

Fiber Fads

Apple Oat Bran Muffins

These moist, sweet muffins are a great alternative to dry breakfast cereal. Loaded with raisins and apple slices, they're so delicious that you may forget that just two of them give you a half-cup of oat bran.

1 medium-size tart green-skinned apple, such as Granny Smith
1 tablespoon lemon juice
2½ cups oat bran
1 tablespoon baking powder
1½ teaspoons ground cinnamon
¼ teaspoon ground nutmeg
⅛ teaspoon ground cloves
1 cup unsweetened applesauce
½ cup nonfat milk
¼ cup firmly packed brown sugar
2 egg whites
2 tablespoons salad oil
½ cup raisins

Peel and core apple; cut into thin slices and toss in a small bowl with lemon juice. Set aside.

In a large bowl, stir together oat bran, baking powder, cinnamon, nutmeg, and cloves. In another bowl, mix applesauce, milk, sugar, egg whites, oil, raisins, and apple slices; add to dry ingredients. Stir just until evenly moistened. Spoon batter into greased or paper-lined 2½-inch muffin cups.

Bake in a 425° oven until a wooden pick inserted in center of muffins comes out clean (about 15 minutes). Makes 10 muffins.

■

Per muffin: 176 calories (23% fat, 64% carbohydrates, 13% protein), 5 g total fat, .4 g saturated fat, .2 mg cholesterol, 29 g carbohydrates, 6 g protein, 148 mg sodium

---

Claims of health benefits can give a food widespread popularity. The demand for fiber-rich foods, for example, stems from studies showing a link between certain types of fiber and lowered blood cholesterol.

There are two kinds of dietary fiber: water-insoluble and water-soluble. Water-insoluble fiber is contained in whole wheat products, fruits, and vegetables; water-soluble fiber—the type that helps reduce cholesterol—is found in dry beans and peas, oats, and rice bran.

Of course, concentrating on high-fiber foods alone won't guarantee you good health; there is no substitute for a balanced diet low in cholesterol and saturated fat. Nonetheless, you can capitalize on the increased availability of fiber-rich foods; just read ingredient labels carefully (see "How To Read a Label," page 109) to make sure the emphasis is on less fat and cholesterol as well as more fiber. Dishes like our Black Bean Salad and Apple Oat Bran Muffins are all-around valuable choices for a healthful diet.

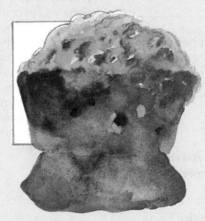

Black Bean Salad

Red bell pepper, yellow lemon peel, and green onions accent this zesty black bean salad.

1¾ cups dried black beans (about ½ lb.)
8 cups regular-strength chicken broth, Chicken-Vegetable Stock (page 76), or water
½ teaspoon ground red pepper (cayenne)
1 small red bell pepper, seeded and finely chopped
½ cup diagonally sliced green onions (including tops)
2 tablespoons balsamic vinegar or red wine vinegar
1 tablespoon *each* lemon juice and very thinly slivered lemon peel
½ cup firmly packed fresh cilantro (coriander) sprigs
Salt

Sort beans to remove any debris; rinse and drain beans, then place in a 4- to 5-quart pan and add broth and ¼ teaspoon of the red pepper. Bring to a boil over high heat. Reduce heat, cover, and simmer until beans are tender to bite but still firm (about 45 minutes). Pour beans into a strainer. Rinse under cold water until water runs clear and beans are cool; eat one to test (about 3 minutes). Drain well.

In a bowl, mix beans, bell pepper, onions, vinegar, lemon juice, lemon peel, and remaining ¼ teaspoon red pepper. Reserve several cilantro sprigs; chop remaining cilantro and stir into salad. Season to taste with salt. Garnish with reserved cilantro sprigs. Makes 6 to 8 servings.

■

Per serving: 135 calories (17% fat, 59% carbohydrates, 24% protein), 3 g total fat, .1 g saturated fat, 0 mg cholesterol, 21 g carbohydrates, 9 g protein, 1007 mg sodium

White Bean & Cherry Tomato Salad

Per serving:
187 **calories** (16% fat, 63% carbohydrates, 21% protein),
3 g **total fat**, .5 g **saturated fat**, 0 mg **cholesterol**,
30 g **carbohydrates**, 10 g **protein**, 274 mg **sodium**

Preparation time: About 15 minutes, plus 1 hour to soak beans

Cooking time: About 1 hour

Chilling time: At least 6 hours

Take this cool, colorful salad of beans and tomatoes in a mustard vinaigrette on your next picnic; it can be made up to a day ahead. Soaking the beans before simmering them cuts the cooking time.

- 1 **pound dried small white beans**
- 1 **teaspoon salt**
- 2 **tablespoons white wine vinegar**
- 1 **tablespoon Dijon mustard**
- 4 **drops liquid hot pepper seasoning**
- 2 **tablespoons salad oil**
- 2 **tablespoons chopped fresh basil leaves or 2 teaspoons dry basil**
- 1½ **teaspoons chopped fresh mint leaves or ½ teaspoon dry mint**
- 3 **tablespoons *each* chopped parsley and green onions (including tops)**
- 1 **small clove garlic, minced or pressed**
- 2 **cups cherry tomatoes, halved**
- 1 **large red bell pepper, seeded and chopped Fresh mint sprigs**

Sort beans to remove any debris. Rinse and drain beans. In a 4- to 5-quart pan, bring 8 cups water to a boil over high heat. Add beans and cook, uncovered, for 2 minutes. Remove from heat, cover, and let stand for 1 hour. Drain beans.

In same pan, combine salt and 6 cups water; bring to a boil over high heat. Add beans, partially cover, and cook until tender to bite (about 1 hour). Drain and set aside.

In a bowl, combine vinegar, mustard, and hot pepper seasoning. Beating constantly with a whisk, slowly add oil; then set dressing aside.

In a large bowl, combine beans, basil, chopped mint, parsley, onions, and garlic. Mix in dressing. Cover and refrigerate for at least 6 hours or up to 1 day. Just before serving, lightly mix in tomatoes and bell pepper; garnish with mint sprigs. Makes 8 to 10 servings.

Baked Lentils with Cheese

Per serving:
295 **calories** (10% fat, 63% carbohydrates, 27% protein),
3 g **total fat**, 2 g **saturated fat**, 7 mg **cholesterol**,
47 g **carbohydrates**, 20 g **protein**, 934 mg **sodium**

Preparation time: About 15 minutes

Baking time: About 1¼ hours

Here's the perfect meal for a chilly winter day. As the lentils and vegetables bake together in a covered casserole, their flavors blend.

- 2 **cups (about 12 oz.) lentils with skins**
- 2 **cups water**
- 1 **bay leaf**
- 2 **teaspoons salt**
- ¼ **teaspoon *each* pepper, dry marjoram leaves, rubbed sage, and dry thyme leaves**
- 2 **large onions, chopped**
- 2 **cloves garlic, minced or pressed**
- 1 **can (about 14 oz.) tomatoes**
- ¾ **pound carrots, cut into ⅛-inch-thick slices**
- 1 **stalk celery, thinly sliced**
- 1 **medium-size green bell pepper, seeded and chopped**
- 2 **tablespoons chopped parsley**
- ⅓ **cup shredded extra-sharp Cheddar cheese**

Sort lentils to remove any debris; then rinse and drain lentils and place them in a shallow 3-quart casserole or 9- by 13-inch baking dish. Add water, bay leaf, salt, pepper, marjoram, sage, thyme, onions, garlic, and tomatoes (break up with a spoon) and their liquid.

Cover and bake in a 375° oven for 30 minutes. Remove from oven and stir in carrots and celery. Cover and continue to bake until vegetables are tender (about 40 more minutes). Remove from oven and stir in bell pepper and parsley; sprinkle with cheese. Return to oven and continue to bake, uncovered, until cheese is melted (about 5 more minutes). Makes 6 servings.

Barley & Lentils with Mint

Per serving:
315 **calories** (14% fat, 67% carbohydrates, 19% protein), 5 g **total fat**, .6 g **saturated fat**, 0 mg **cholesterol**, 54 g **carbohydrates**, 16 g **protein**, 44 mg **sodium**

Preparation time: About 10 minutes

Cooking time: About 45 minutes

Barley and lentils mixed with yogurt and fresh mint make a refreshing side dish for an Indian-influenced meal. If you use decorticated (skinless) lentils, watch them closely; they'll get mushy if cooked too long.

- 1 **cup (about 6 oz.) lentils, with skins or decorticated**
- 1 **cup pearl barley**
- 4 **cups low-sodium chicken broth**
- ½ **cup** *each* **raisins and minced fresh mint**
- ¼ **cup whole blanched almonds**
- 1 **cup lowfat plain yogurt (optional)**

Sort lentils to remove any debris. Rinse and drain lentils and barley. In a 2- to 3-quart pan, bring broth to a boil. Add barley and lentils (if using lentils with skins). Reduce heat, cover, and simmer until barley and lentils are tender to bite (about 40 minutes); drain. (If using decorticated lentils, add when barley is almost tender—after about 30 minutes; continue to cook just until lentils and barley are tender to bite, about 10 more minutes.) Stir raisins and mint into lentils and barley, then pour into a serving bowl.

While lentils and barley are cooking, toast almonds in a 350° oven until golden (about 8 minutes), stirring several times. Sprinkle almonds over lentil-barley mixture. Offer yogurt to add to taste, if desired. Makes 6 servings.

Pictured on facing page

Black Bean Tacos

Per serving:
390 **calories** (30% fat, 54% carbohydrates, 16% protein), 13 g **total fat**, 2 g **saturated fat**, 6 mg **cholesterol**, 55 g **carbohydrates**, 17 g **protein**, 719 mg **sodium**

Preparation time: About 15 minutes, plus 1 hour to soak beans

Cooking time: About 2½ hours

For a filling meatless main course, fold soft flour tortillas around spicy black beans and spoonfuls of salad tossed with chili-cumin dressing, then top with cheese and cool yogurt. Using extra-sharp Cheddar lets you add more flavor with less fat.

- **Black Beans (recipe follows)**
- 12 **flour tortillas (***each*** about 8 inches in diameter)**
- 1 **head romaine lettuce (about 1 lb.), cut into shreds**
- 1 **large tomato, chopped**
- 1 **large red bell pepper, seeded and cut into strips**
- 6 **green onions (including tops), thinly sliced**
- ¼ **cup red wine vinegar**
- 1 **large clove garlic, minced or pressed**
- 1 **teaspoon chili powder**
- ½ **teaspoon** *each* **ground cumin and salt**
- ¼ **teaspoon pepper**
- 2 **tablespoons olive oil or salad oil**
- ¼ **cup shredded extra-sharp Cheddar cheese**
- 1 **cup nonfat plain yogurt**

Prepare beans; keep warm. Stack tortillas, wrap in foil, and heat in a 350° oven for 15 minutes.

Meanwhile, place lettuce, tomato, bell pepper, and onions in a large salad bowl. Then prepare dressing: combine vinegar, garlic, chili powder, cumin, salt, and pepper; add oil and blend well.

To serve, toss salad with dressing. To assemble a taco, spoon ¼ cup beans into a tortilla; add about ½ cup salad, 1 teaspoon cheese, and 1⅓ tablespoons yogurt. Makes 6 servings.

Black Beans. Sort 1 cup **dried black beans** to remove any debris. Rinse and drain beans. In a 3-quart pan, bring 4 cups **water** to a boil. Add beans; boil for 2 minutes. Remove from heat, cover, and let stand for 1 hour. Drain and rinse beans.

Heat 1 tablespoon **olive oil** in a 3-quart pan over medium heat. Add 1 large **onion,** chopped; cook, stirring occasionally, until soft (about 10 minutes). Add beans, 1 clove **garlic** (minced), **1 small dried hot red chile** (crushed), ½ teaspoon **salt,** and 2½ cups **water.** Bring to a boil over high heat. Reduce heat, cover, and simmer until liquid is absorbed and beans are very tender (about 2 hours).

*Pile on the goodies! That's what we've done with our Black Bean Tacos
(recipe on facing page). Flour tortillas are stuffed with simmered black beans,
chili-seasoned salad, shredded cheese, and cooling yogurt.*

63

Fruits & Vegetables

Everyone knows that vegetables and fruits are good for you:

they're high in minerals, fiber, and vitamins (especially

A and C); they're cholesterol-free and low in sodium; and

almost all are very low in fat (coconuts, avocados, and olives

are exceptions). And besides all that—they taste good.

If you grew up on boiled carrots and canned spinach, you'll

be surprised and delighted at the wonderfully sweet, fresh

flavors of properly cooked vegetables, here presented in a

variety of lowfat sauces and dressings. With the tempting

choices offered in this chapter, healthful eating is easy!

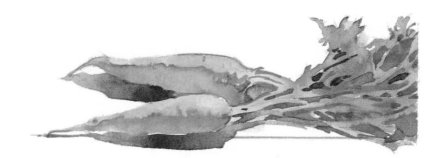

Sweet & Sour Broccoli

Per serving:
36 *calories* (5% fat, 75% carbohydrates, 20% protein),
.2 g *total fat*, 0 g *saturated fat*, 0 mg *cholesterol*,
8 g *carbohydrates*, 2 g *protein*, 66 mg *sodium*

Preparation time: About 10 minutes

Cooking time: 5 to 8 minutes

It takes next to no time to dress up steamed broccoli deliciously for dinner—just toss with rice vinegar, soy sauce, and a little sugar.

About 1 pound broccoli
½ **cup unseasoned rice vinegar**
1 **tablespoon sugar**
½ **teaspoon soy sauce**

Cut stalks from broccoli; peel stalks, then cut diagonally into ¼-inch-thick slices. Cut flowerets into bite-size pieces. Arrange all broccoli on a rack and steam over boiling water just until tender when pierced (5 to 8 minutes). Turn into a large bowl.

In a small bowl, combine vinegar, sugar, and soy; pour over warm broccoli and mix well. Drain immediately and serve. Makes 4 servings.

Red Cabbage with Apple

Per serving:
141 *calories* (24% fat, 68% carbohydrates, 8% protein),
4 g *total fat*, .5 g *saturated fat*, 0 mg *cholesterol*,
26 g *carbohydrates*, 3 g *protein*, 22 mg *sodium*

Preparation time: About 10 minutes

Cooking time: About 1 hour

Perfect fare for a cold winter evening, this tempting sweet-tart dish combines shredded cabbage and apples with brown sugar, vinegar, and caraway seeds.

1 **tablespoon salad oil**
1 **large onion, thinly sliced**
1 **medium-size head red cabbage (about 1½ lbs.), shredded**
1 **medium-size tart apple, peeled, cored, and shredded**
1 **large clove garlic, minced or pressed**
1 **teaspoon caraway seeds**
2 **tablespoons firmly packed brown sugar**
½ **cup red wine vinegar**
1 **cup water**

Heat oil in a 12- to 14-inch frying pan over medium heat; add onion and cook, stirring, until soft (about 10 minutes). Add cabbage and apple and cook, stirring, for 5 minutes. Stir in garlic, caraway seeds, sugar, vinegar, and water. Bring to a boil; reduce heat, cover, and simmer, stirring occasionally, until cabbage is very tender and almost all liquid has evaporated (about 45 minutes). Makes 4 servings.

Dress up your dinner menu with a special side dish—rosemary-accented Stir-fried Carrots & Peppers (recipe on facing page). Quick cooking in a tiny bit of oil helps preserve the flavor, texture, and color of the vegetable strips.

Pictured on facing page

Stir-fried Carrots & Peppers

Preparation time: About 15 minutes

Cooking time: About 8 minutes

Thin strips of carrots, red bell pepper, and fresh green chiles mingle in this bright-colored vegetable sauté.

- **1 tablespoon olive oil**
- **1½ pounds carrots, cut into matchstick pieces**
- **1 medium-size red bell pepper, seeded and cut into matchstick pieces**
- **2 medium-size fresh Anaheim (California) chiles, seeded and cut into matchstick pieces**
- **2 teaspoons fresh rosemary leaves or 1 teaspoon dry rosemary**
  Pepper

Per serving:
*76 **calories** (28% fat, 65% carbohydrates, 7% protein), 3 g **total fat**, .3 g **saturated fat**, 0 mg **cholesterol**, 13 g **carbohydrates**, 1 g **protein**, 41 mg **sodium***

Heat oil in a 10- to 12-inch frying pan over medium-high heat; add carrots and cook, stirring, just until lightly browned (about 6 minutes). Add bell pepper, chiles, and rosemary; cook, stirring, until pepper pieces are limp (about 2 minutes). Season to taste with pepper. Makes 6 servings.

Vegetable Kebabs

Preparation time: About 15 minutes

Marinating time: At least 2 hours

Cooking time: About 40 minutes

Surprise guests at your next barbecue with an unusual side dish: skewered herb-marinated vegetables.

- **1 small eggplant (about ¾ lb.), unpeeled, cut into 2-inch cubes**
- **½ pound carrots, cut into ½-inch-thick slices**
  About 12 small thin-skinned potatoes (*each* 1½ to 2 inches in diameter)
- **1 pound zucchini, cut into 1-inch-thick slices**
- **2 small red or green bell peppers, seeded and cut into 1-inch squares**
- **1 large onion, cut into wedges and layers separated**
  About 16 large whole mushrooms
  Herb Marinade (recipe follows)

In a 4- to 5-quart pan, cook eggplant in 1 inch of boiling water for 3 minutes; drain. Cook carrots in 1 inch of boiling water until tender-crisp to bite

Per serving:
*357 **calories** (28% fat, 62% carbohydrates, 10% protein), 12 g **total fat**, 1 g **saturated fat**, 0 mg **cholesterol**, 58 g **carbohydrates**, 10 g **protein**, 77 mg **sodium***

(about 7 minutes); drain. Cook unpeeled potatoes in 1 inch of boiling water just until tender when pierced (about 20 minutes); drain and cut in half.

Place eggplant, carrots, potatoes, zucchini, bell peppers, onion, and mushrooms in a plastic bag. Prepare Herb Marinade; pour over vegetables. Seal bag, set in a shallow pan, and refrigerate for at least 2 hours or until next day, turning bag occasionally.

Drain marinade from vegetables; reserve. Thread vegetables alternately on 8 sturdy metal skewers. Place on a lightly greased grill 4 to 6 inches above a solid bed of low coals. Cook, turning and basting often with marinade, until all vegetables are tender when pierced (about 10 minutes). Makes 4 servings.

Herb Marinade. In a food processor or blender, combine 1 large **onion** (cut into chunks); 2 cloves **garlic**; ½ teaspoon **pepper**; ¼ cup **white wine vinegar**; ½ cup **dry white wine**; 2 tablespoons **salad oil**; 1 teaspoon *each* **dry thyme leaves, dry rosemary**, grated **lemon peel**, and **honey**; and 1 tablespoon **lemon juice**. Whirl until onion is puréed.

Coriander-spiced Eggplant

Per serving:

*61 **calories** (25% fat, 64% carbohydrates, 11% protein), 2 g **total fat**, .2 g **saturated fat**, 0 mg **cholesterol**, 11 g **carbohydrates**, 2 g **protein**, 376 mg **sodium***

Preparation time: About 15 minutes

Cooking time: About 1½ hours

The problem with sautéing eggplant is that it tends to soak up oil like a sponge. To save fat and calories, we've baked this eggplant in a hot oven, then mixed the diced pulp into a spicy curry-seasoned sauce made with just 2 teaspoons of olive oil.

- 1 **large or 2 small eggplants (1½ to 2 lbs.** *total***)**
- 2 **teaspoons olive oil or salad oil**
- ½ **teaspoon cumin seeds**
- 1 **tablespoon minced fresh ginger**
- 1 **small red onion, thickly sliced**
- 1 **teaspoon ground turmeric**
- 1 **medium-size green bell pepper, seeded and coarsely chopped**
- 2 **teaspoons ground coriander**
- 1 **teaspoon** *each* **ground cumin, paprika, and salt**
- ¼ **teaspoon pepper**
- 1 **large tomato, peeled and chopped**
- ¼ **cup water**
- ¼ **cup coarsely chopped fresh cilantro (coriander)**

Place whole unpeeled eggplant in a rimmed 10- by 15-inch baking pan and bake in a 400° oven until very soft (about 50 minutes). Let cool slightly, then cut a slit in eggplant and scoop out pulp; discard large seed pockets, skin, and stem. Coarsely chop pulp; place in a colander to drain.

Heat oil in a 12- to 14-inch frying pan over medium heat. Add cumin seeds, ginger, and onion; cook, stirring occasionally, until onion is soft (about 10 minutes). Stir in turmeric, bell pepper, coriander, ground cumin, paprika, salt, pepper, and tomato. Cook, stirring occasionally, until tomato has released its juice (about 5 minutes). Add water and bring to a simmer. Reduce heat to low and simmer, uncovered, for 10 minutes. Add chopped eggplant and cook until hot (about 5 minutes). Remove from heat, add cilantro, and serve. Makes 6 servings.

Glazed Onions

Per serving:

*166 **calories** (19% fat, 77% carbohydrates, 4% protein), 4 g **total fat**, .5 g **saturated fat**, 0 mg **cholesterol**, 34 g **carbohydrates**, 2 g **protein**, 11 mg **sodium***

Preparation time: About 20 minutes

Cooking time: About 25 minutes

Warning: Not for the timid! Combined with sweet currants in a dark, tangy Madeira sauce, these small onions pack a powerful punch. Serve them alongside any mild-flavored main course.

- 1½ **cups Madeira or port**
- ¾ **cup distilled white vinegar**
- ½ **cup firmly packed brown sugar**
- ½ **cup currants or raisins**
- ⅛ **teaspoon ground red pepper (cayenne)**
- 2 **pounds small white boiling onions (***each* **1 to 1½ inches in diameter), peeled**
- 2 **tablespoons salad oil**

In a 3- to 4-quart pan, combine Madeira, vinegar, sugar, currants, and red pepper. Bring to a boil over high heat; boil rapidly, uncovered, until reduced to 1¼ cups (about 7 minutes). Set aside.

In a 12- to 14-inch frying pan, arrange as many onions as will fit in a single layer. Pour oil over onions. Cook over medium heat until lightly browned (about 5 minutes), shaking pan to turn onions. With a slotted spoon, transfer browned onions to Madeira sauce. Repeat with any remaining onions.

Bring onions in sauce to a boil over high heat; reduce heat, cover, and simmer until onions are tender-crisp when pierced (about 10 minutes). Remove from heat and let cool. Serve warm or at room temperature. Makes 6 to 8 servings.

Baked New Potatoes & Apples

Per serving:

162 **calories** (20% fat, 74% carbohydrates, 6% protein), 4 g **total fat**, .4 g **saturated fat**, 0 mg **cholesterol**, 31 g **carbohydrates**, 3 g **protein**, 124 mg **sodium**

Preparation time: About 15 minutes

Baking time: About 50 minutes

Potatoes and apples are classic partners. Here, small whole potatoes and red apple wedges slowly bake together in a flavorful sauce of beef broth, apple juice, and allspice.

    2 pounds small thin-skinned potatoes (*each* 1½ to 2 inches in diameter)
    2 medium-size onions, cut into 1-inch wedges
    2 tablespoons olive oil
    1 pound red-skinned apples, such as Winesap, Jonathan, or Empire
    1¼ cups regular-strength beef broth
    ¾ cup apple juice
    2 tablespoons cornstarch
    ¾ teaspoon ground allspice

Place unpeeled potatoes in a 9- by 13-inch baking pan. Break apart onion wedges and sprinkle over potatoes. Add oil and mix well. Bake, uncovered, in a 400° oven for 25 minutes; stir occasionally.

Meanwhile, quarter and core apples, then cut into ¾-inch wedges. In a small bowl, combine broth, apple juice, cornstarch, and allspice.

When potatoes have baked for 25 minutes, mix in juice mixture and apples. Return to oven and continue to bake, spooning juices over apples and potatoes several times, until potatoes are very tender when pierced and juices begin to form thick bubbles (about 25 more minutes). Makes 8 or 9 servings.

Golden Acorn Squash

Per serving:

197 **calories** (25% fat, 71% carbohydrates, 4% protein), 6 g **total fat**, 1 g **saturated fat**, 0 mg **cholesterol**, 38 g **carbohydrates**, 2 g **protein**, 77 mg **sodium**

Preparation time: About 5 minutes

Baking time: About 55 minutes

Sweet acorn squash halves filled with hot orange-brandy sauce are a good-looking way to warm up a winter meal.

    2 tablespoons margarine
    2 acorn squash (about 1¼ lbs. *each*), cut in half lengthwise and seeded
    3 tablespoons *each* firmly packed brown sugar and frozen concentrated orange juice, thawed
    3 tablespoons brandy or water
      Orange slices (optional)

Place 1 tablespoon of the margarine in a 9- by 13-inch baking pan. Place pan in a 350° oven to melt margarine; tilt pan to coat bottom. Lay squash halves, cut side down, in pan. Bake, uncovered, in a 350° oven until squash is tender when pierced (about 35 minutes).

Meanwhile, in a 1- to 1½-quart pan, mix remaining 1 tablespoon margarine, sugar, concen-trated orange juice, and brandy. Bring to a boil over high heat, stirring; then set aside.

Turn squash halves cut side up. Pour brandy mixture evenly into each half. Continue to bake until edges of squash are browned (about 15 more minutes). Transfer squash to a platter or plates, taking care not to spill sauce. Garnish with orange slices, if desired. Makes 4 servings.

Vegetable Curry

Per serving:

117 **calories** *(19% fat, 69% carbohydrates, 12% protein),*
3 g **total fat**, *.3 g* **saturated fat**, *0 mg* **cholesterol,**
23 g **carbohydrates**, *4 g* **protein**, *34 mg* **sodium**

Preparation time: About 20 minutes

Cooking time: About 35 minutes

Curry powder and other curry spices flavor this combination of eight different vegetables. Serve it with warmed pocket bread and your choice of condiments—perhaps raisins, chutney, and cool yogurt.

- 1 **tablespoon olive oil or salad oil**
- 1 **large onion, coarsely chopped**
- ½ **pound broccoli**
- 1 **teaspoon curry powder**
- ½ **teaspoon black pepper**
- ¼ **teaspoon** *each* **ground ginger and ground cumin**
- ⅛ **teaspoon ground red pepper (cayenne)**
- 2 **bay leaves**
- ½ **pound carrots, cut into ¼-inch-thick slices**
- ½ **pound green beans, cut into 2-inch lengths**
- 1 **red or green bell pepper, seeded and cut into 1-inch pieces**
- ⅓ **pound cauliflowerets**
- ½ **pound butternut or banana squash, peeled and cut into 1-inch pieces**
- ½ **pound thin-skinned potatoes, unpeeled, cut into 1-inch chunks**
- ¾ **cup water**

Heat oil in a 5-quart pan over medium heat. Add onion and cook, stirring occasionally, until soft (about 10 minutes). Meanwhile, cut stalks from broccoli; peel stalks, then cut into ½-inch-thick slices. Separate flowerets; set all broccoli aside.

To onion, add curry powder, black pepper, ginger, cumin, and red pepper; cook for 1 minute. Add bay leaves, broccoli, carrots, beans, bell pepper, cauliflowerets, squash, potatoes, and water. Cover and bring to a boil; reduce heat and simmer until vegetables are just tender when pierced (about 20 minutes). Uncover, increase heat to high, and cook until sauce is thickened (about 5 minutes). Remove bay leaves before serving. Makes 6 servings.

Spinach-stuffed Tomatoes

Per serving:

99 **calories** *(30% fat, 51% carbohydrates, 19% protein),*
4 g **total fat**, *1 g* **saturated fat**, *3 mg* **cholesterol,**
14 g **carbohydrates**, *5 g* **protein**, *167 mg* **sodium**

Preparation time: About 25 minutes

Cooking time: About 15 minutes

Fancy enough for company: red tomatoes stuffed with deep green, nutmeg-scented spinach filling and dusted with Parmesan cheese. You won't need the tops of the tomatoes for this dish; save them to dice for salsa or salads.

- 8 **medium-size tomatoes**
- 1 **tablespoon olive oil or salad oil**
- 1 **large onion, chopped**
- 1 **pound cleaned spinach, coarsely chopped**
- ½ **cup fine dry bread crumbs**
- ¼ **cup grated Parmesan cheese**
- ¼ **teaspoon ground nutmeg**

Cut off top fourth of each tomato; reserve for other uses. With a small spoon, scoop out pulp to make hollow shells. Chop pulp; let drain in a colander.

Heat oil in a 10- to 12-inch frying pan over medium-high heat. Add onion; cook, stirring, until soft (about 7 minutes). Stir in drained tomato pulp and spinach; cook, stirring, until spinach is wilted (about 3 minutes). Stir in bread crumbs, 2 tablespoons of the cheese, and nutmeg.

Fill tomatoes with spinach mixture and arrange in an ungreased baking pan. Sprinkle evenly with remaining 2 tablespoons cheese. Broil 4 inches below heat until cheese is lightly browned (about 3 minutes). Makes 8 servings.

Vegetable Curry (recipe on facing page) offers a bountiful feast: carrots, cauliflower, squash, potatoes, broccoli, green beans, and bell pepper simmered in a delicate spice blend.

Napa Cabbage Salad

Per serving:
59 calories (3% fat, 88% carbohydrates, 9% protein),
.2 g total fat, 0 g saturated fat, 0 mg cholesterol,
14 g carbohydrates, 1 g protein, 31 mg sodium

Preparation time: About 10 minutes

Napa cabbage, pale green in color and correspondingly delicate in flavor, is delicious in salads. Here, it's combined with shredded carrots, minced garlic, and ginger in a simple slaw that can be made several hours ahead.

- 1 **pound carrots, finely shredded**
- 4 **cups finely slivered napa cabbage**
- ⅓ **cup white wine vinegar**
- 2 **tablespoons sugar**
- 1 **clove garlic, minced**
- 1 **teaspoon minced fresh ginger**
  Salt

In a serving bowl, gently mix carrots, cabbage, vinegar, sugar, garlic, and ginger; season to taste with salt. Serve at once; or, if made ahead, cover and refrigerate for up to 4 hours. Serve cold or at room temperature. Makes 6 servings.

Cherry Salad with Orange Dressing

Per serving:
240 calories (12% fat, 78% carbohydrates, 10% protein),
4 g total fat, .7 g saturated fat, .8 mg cholesterol,
51 g carbohydrates, 6 g protein, 130 mg sodium

Preparation time: About 30 minutes

Bright colors and buoyant flavors are well matched in this cool salad. A sesame-accented yogurt dressing tops ripe pineapple and dark, glossy cherries.

- **Orange Dressing (recipe follows)**
- 1 **medium-size head iceberg lettuce**
- 1 **small pineapple (about 2½ lbs.), peeled, cored, and cut into 1-inch chunks**
- 2½ **cups dark sweet cherries (about 1 lb.), stemmed and pitted**

Prepare Orange Dressing; set aside.

Line a 1½- to 2-quart bowl with about 4 of the largest lettuce leaves. Break remaining lettuce into bite-size pieces and place in bowl. Add pineapple and cherries. Pour dressing over salad and mix to coat evenly. Makes about 6 servings.

Orange Dressing. Toast 2 tablespoons **sesame seeds** in a small frying pan over medium heat until golden (about 3 minutes), shaking pan frequently. In a bowl, stir together 1 cup **nonfat plain yogurt,** 3 tablespoons *each* **lime juice** and **frozen concentrated orange juice** (thawed), and ¼ teaspoon **salt.** Add sesame seeds; stir until blended.

Fig & Prosciutto Salad

Per serving:

153 calories (10% fat, 76% carbohydrates, 14% protein), 2 g total fat, .7 g saturated fat, 8 mg cholesterol, 31 g carbohydrates, 6 g protein, 179 mg sodium

Preparation time: About 10 minutes

A lemony yogurt dressing accented with fresh mint enhances this favorite combination of fruit and meat.

- ½ **cup** *each* **lowfat lemon yogurt and nonfat plain yogurt**
- 1 **tablespoon shredded fresh mint**
- 12 **small or 6 large figs, stems trimmed**
- 4 **thin slices lean prosciutto (about 1½ oz.** *total)*
  Fresh mint sprigs

In a small bowl, blend lemon yogurt, plain yogurt, and shredded mint. Cut small figs vertically in halves; cut large figs into quarters. Cut prosciutto slices in half crosswise; roll up each piece.

Spoon yogurt mixture equally into centers of 4 salad plates. Divide figs and prosciutto evenly among plates, arranging figs cut side up atop dressing. Garnish with mint sprigs and serve at once. Makes 4 servings.

Pictured on front cover

Golden Pepper Salad

Per serving:

113 calories (20% fat, 63% carbohydrates, 17% protein), 3 g total fat, .3 g saturated fat, 0 mg cholesterol, 19 g carbohydrates, 5 g protein, 241 mg sodium

Preparation time: About 25 minutes

One sweet yellow bell pepper goes into this mixed green salad; another is puréed for the dressing. If you like, substitute other favorite mild and sharp greens for those suggested below.

- **Golden Dressing (recipe follows)**
- 1 **head red leaf lettuce (about ½ lb.)**
- 1 **small head red oak leaf lettuce (about ¼ lb.)**
- 1 **small head chicory (about ¾ lb.)**
- 1 **large bunch watercress (about ½ lb.)**
- 1 **head Belgian endive (about ¼ lb.)**
- 1 *each* **medium-size yellow and red bell pepper**
- 1 **can (about 1 lb.) garbanzo beans, drained**

Prepare Golden Dressing; set aside.

In a 3- to 4-quart bowl, combine red leaf lettuce (tear larger leaves in half), oak leaf lettuce, and inner leaves of chicory (discard outer leaves).

Remove tough stems from watercress; add leaves and small sprigs to bowl.

Cut endive in half lengthwise, then cut each half crosswise into thin strips. Cut yellow and red bell peppers in half lengthwise; remove seeds, then cut each pepper half crosswise into thin strips. Add endive, bell peppers, and garbanzos to bowl of greens.

Stir Golden Dressing to blend, pour over salad, and mix gently. Makes 8 servings.

Golden Dressing. In a blender or food processor, combine 1 tablespoon **olive oil,** ½ cup diced **yellow bell pepper,** 1 tablespoon minced **shallot,** and ⅛ teaspoon *each* **salt** and **ground red pepper** (cayenne). Whirl until smoothly puréed. (At this point, you may cover and refrigerate until next day.) Just before serving, thoroughly blend in 2 tablespoons **white wine vinegar.**

At teatime or for a light lunch, enjoy currant-studded Marjoram Scones (recipe on page 81) and refreshing Nectarine Salad Ring (recipe on facing page) with tall glasses of icy lemonade.

Tropical Jicama Salad

Per serving:

*180 **calories** (23% fat, 66% carbohydrates, 11% protein), 5 g **total fat**, .5 g **saturated fat**, .8 mg **cholesterol**, 32 g **carbohydrates**, 6 g **protein**, 55 mg **sodium***

Preparation time: About 25 minutes

Crisp jicama tastes something like a cross between an apple and a sweet turnip—and it goes well with fruits as well as vegetables. Here, it's tossed with pineapple, papaya, celery, yogurt, and crunchy almonds.

- 1 **medium-size jicama (about 1¼ lbs.), peeled and cut into ⅛-inch-thick matchstick pieces**
- 2 **cups small fresh or canned pineapple chunks**
- 1 **medium-size firm-ripe papaya (about 1 lb.), peeled, seeded, and diced**
- 1 **cup thinly sliced celery**
- ¼ **cup whole blanched almonds**
- 2 **teaspoons salad oil**
- ½ **cup currants or raisins**
- 1 **teaspoon curry powder**
- 1 **cup nonfat plain yogurt**

In a large bowl, combine jicama, pineapple, papaya, and celery. (At this point, you may cover and refrigerate for up to 4 hours.)

Toast almonds in a 10- to 12-inch frying pan over medium heat until golden brown (about 5 minutes), stirring frequently. Set aside. Pour oil into pan and add currants and curry powder; stir over medium heat until currants are puffed (about 2 minutes). Remove from heat, combine with almonds, and let cool. Stir yogurt into jicama mixture, then spoon almond mixture over salad. Makes 6 servings.

Pictured on facing page

Nectarine Salad Ring

Per serving:

*148 **calories** (5% fat, 86% carbohydrates, 9% protein), .9 g **total fat**, .2 g **saturated fat**, 2 mg **cholesterol**, 34 g **carbohydrates**, 4 g **protein**, 48 mg **sodium***

Preparation time: About 20 minutes

Chilling time: About 4½ hours

Welcome summer with a simple fresh fruit mold that's as attractive as it is appetizing. Blueberries and rosy-skinned nectarine slices float in a ring of honey-sweetened gelatin.

- 1 **envelope unflavored gelatin**
- 1 **cup lowfat buttermilk**
- 1 **cup orange juice**
- ¼ **cup honey**
- 3½ **cups sliced nectarines**
- 2 **cups blueberries**

In a blender or food processor, sprinkle gelatin over buttermilk; let soften for 5 minutes. In a small pan, bring orange juice to a boil; add orange juice and honey to gelatin mixture, then whirl until blended. Pour mixture into a bowl; cover and refrigerate until thick and syrupy (about 30 minutes).

Stir nectarines and blueberries into gelatin mixture; pour into a 1½-quart mold. Cover and refrigerate until firm (about 4 hours).

To serve, dip mold to rim in warm water for 10 seconds; run tip of a knife around edge to loosen Invert onto a serving plate; lift off mold. Makes 4 to 6 servings.

Make It Yourself

One way to limit fat and cholesterol in your diet is to make your own dressings and toppings. Toss fresh green salads with our Spicy French Dressing, made with oil low in saturated fat; olive oil and canola oil are both good choices for this tangy-sweet vinaigrette. Rather than covering your desserts with whipped cream, spoon on our fat-free Whipped Topping made with nonfat dry milk. We also include instructions for a lowfat, low-sodium Chicken-Vegetable Stock; use it in any recipe that doesn't require a clear broth.

Spicy French Dressing

½ cup *each* sugar and cider vinegar
1 tablespoon all-purpose flour
1 teaspoon *each* salt and Worcestershire
1 medium-size onion, finely chopped
1 clove garlic, minced or pressed
2 tablespoons salad oil or olive oil
⅓ cup catsup
1 teaspoon celery seeds

In a small pan, stir together sugar, vinegar, and flour. Cook over medium heat, stirring, until bubbly and thick. Pour into a blender and add salt, Worcestershire, onion, and garlic; whirl until smooth. With blender on lowest speed, slowly pour in oil in a thin, steady stream, whirling until blended.

Transfer mixture to a bowl and stir in catsup and celery seeds. If made ahead, cover and refrigerate for up to a month. Makes about 2 cups.

■

Per tablespoon: 25 calories (30% fat, 69% carbohydrates, 1% protein), .9 g total fat, .1 g saturated fat, 0 mg cholesterol, 4 g carbohydrates, .1 g protein, 100 mg sodium

Whipped Topping

¾ cup ice water
⅔ cup instant nonfat dry milk powder
¼ cup sugar
1 teaspoon vanilla

Refrigerate beaters and large bowl of an electric mixer until very cold. In chilled mixer bowl, combine ice water and dry milk. Beat on high speed until mixture holds soft peaks (about 5 minutes); if mixture spatters, drape a towel or wax paper loosely over bowl and beaters. Gradually add sugar, beating constantly. Scrape down bowl sides, then add vanilla; continue to beat for 1 more minute. Serve immediately. Makes about 4 cups.

■

Per tablespoon: 6 calories (0% fat, 83% carbohydrates, 17% protein), 0 g total fat, 0 g saturated fat, .1 mg cholesterol, 1 g carbohydrates, .2 g protein, 4 mg sodium

Chicken-Vegetable Stock

5 pounds bony chicken pieces, such as wings, backs, necks, and carcasses
2 large onions, cut into chunks
½ pound carrots, cut into chunks
6 to 8 parsley sprigs
½ teaspoon whole black peppercorns
3½ quarts water

Rinse chicken; then place in a 6- to 8-quart pan along with onions, carrots, parsley sprigs, peppercorns, and water. Bring to a boil; then reduce heat, cover, and simmer for 3 hours. Let cool.

Strain broth into a large bowl. Return onions and carrots to broth; discard chicken pieces. Cover broth and refrigerate until fat is solidified (at least 4 hours) or for up to 2 days. Lift off and discard fat. In a food processor or blender, purée broth and vegetables in batches. To store, freeze in 1- to 4-cup portions for up to 2 months. Makes about 10 cups.

■

Per cup: 60 calories (29% fat, 64% carbohydrates, 7% protein), 2 g total fat, 0 g saturated fat, 0 mg cholesterol, 10 g carbohydrates, 1 g protein, 10 mg sodium

Spinach, Date & Orange Salad

Per serving:
*271 **calories** (26% fat, 69% carbohydrates, 5% protein),*
*9 g **total fat**, 1 g **saturated fat**, 0 mg **cholesterol**,*
*51 g **carbohydrates**, 4 g **protein**, 239 mg **sodium***

Preparation time: About 15 minutes

Layer oranges, dates, and almonds atop spinach leaves for this colorful winter salad. A honey-mustard vinaigrette nicely complements the combination.

    Honey Dressing (recipe follows)
 1 **pound spinach, rinsed well, stems removed**
 2 **large oranges, peeled and cut into thin slices**
12 **medium-size dates, pitted and halved**
 1 **tablespoon slivered blanched almonds**

Prepare Honey Dressing and set aside.

Pat spinach dry; then arrange equal portions of spinach on 4 salad plates. Top evenly with oranges, dates, and almonds. (At this point, you may cover and refrigerate for up to 2 hours.) Before serving, stir Honey Dressing, then drizzle over salads. Makes 4 servings.

Honey Dressing. Stir together ¼ cup *each* **honey** and **red wine vinegar,** 2 tablespoons **salad oil,** 1 teaspoon **Dijon mustard,** and ¼ teaspoon *each* **salt** and **pepper.**

Chili Potato Salad

Per serving:
*185 **calories** (25% fat, 67% carbohydrates, 8% protein),*
*5 g **total fat**, .7 g **saturated fat,** 0 mg **cholesterol,**
*33 g **carbohydrates,** 4 g **protein**, 36 mg **sodium***

Preparation time: About 15 minutes

Tired of the same old potato salad? Try this chili-flavored version at your next picnic. Bright with corn and red bell pepper, it's good cold or at room temperature.

    4 **cups diced cooked unpeeled thin-skinned potatoes (1½ lbs. uncooked)**
    1 **can (about 17 oz.) corn kernels, drained**
    ½ **cup *each* sliced celery and chopped red onion**
    ⅔ **cup chopped red bell pepper**
    2 **tablespoons salad oil**
    4 **tablespoons cider vinegar**
    2 **teaspoons chili powder**
    1 **clove garlic, minced**
    ½ **teaspoon liquid hot pepper seasoning**
       Salt and pepper

In a large bowl, combine potatoes, corn, celery, onion, and bell pepper. Add oil, vinegar, chili powder, garlic, and hot pepper seasoning; season to taste with salt and pepper. If made ahead, cover and refrigerate for up to 1 day. Serve cold or at room temperature. Makes 6 servings.

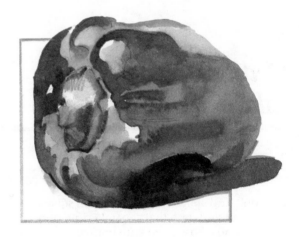

Pictured on facing page

Sweet Potato & Ginger Salad

Preparation time: About 30 minutes

Guests may not be able to guess all the ingredients in this sweet salad, but they're sure to applaud the flavor. If you like, you can prepare the salad several hours in advance.

- ½ **pound sweet potatoes**
- 2 **tablespoons lemon juice**
- 1 **medium-large pineapple (about 4 lbs.)**
- 1 **cup finely shredded peeled jicama**
- 2 **tablespoons salad oil**
- 2 **teaspoons honey**
- 1 **teaspoon** *each* **minced fresh ginger and grated lemon peel**
  Finely chopped parsley
  Red leaf lettuce leaves

Per serving:

244 **calories** *(28% fat, 69% carbohydrates, 3% protein),*
8 g **total fat,** *1 g* **saturated fat,** *0 mg* **cholesterol,**
45 g **carbohydrates,** *2 g* **protein,** *11 mg* **sodium**

In a 5-quart pan, bring about 3 quarts water to a boil over high heat. Peel and shred sweet potatoes; immediately add to boiling water. Cook for 30 seconds, then drain well and mix with lemon juice.

Cut off pineapple peel. Cut about half the pineapple into 4 crosswise slices, cover, and refrigerate. Core and finely chop remaining pineapple; drain briefly in a colander.

Squeeze excess liquid from jicama. Mix jicama, chopped pineapple, oil, honey, ginger, and lemon peel with sweet potatoes. (At this point, you may cover and let stand at room temperature for up to 4 hours.)

To serve, place an equal portion of jicama mixture atop each pineapple slice. Sprinkle with parsley and present on a lettuce-lined platter. Makes 4 servings.

Mediterranean Squash Salad

Preparation time: About 45 minutes

Chilling time: At least 2 hours

You won't find spaghetti in a spaghetti squash—but you will find flesh that separates into thin, tender strands. Toss them with orange juice, currants, and pine nuts for an unusual "pasta" salad.

- 1 **medium-size spaghetti squash (about 3 lbs.)**
- ⅓ **cup currants**
- 2 **tablespoons** *each* **white wine vinegar, orange juice, and firmly packed brown sugar**
- 1 **teaspoon grated orange peel**
- ¼ **cup pine nuts**
  Salt and pepper

Per serving:

95 **calories** *(26% fat, 66% carbohydrates, 8% protein),*
3 g **total fat,** *.5 g* **saturated fat,** *0 mg* **cholesterol,**
17 g **carbohydrates,** *2 g* **protein,** *22 mg* **sodium**

Cut squash in half lengthwise; scoop out and discard seeds. Place squash halves, cut side down, on a rack in a 5- to 6-quart pan (halves can overlap). Fill pan with no more than 2 inches water (enough to come to just below rack). Bring to a boil. Cover and boil steadily until squash pulp is tender when pierced (about 25 minutes); add more boiling water to pan as needed. Let squash cool, then scoop out pulp and separate strands with 2 forks.

In a large bowl, mix currants, vinegar, orange juice, sugar, and orange peel. Add squash; stir to blend. Cover and refrigerate until cold (at least 2 hours) or until next day. Stir pine nuts into squash mixture. Season to taste with salt and pepper. Makes 6 to 8 servings.

There's nothing shy about Sweet Potato & Ginger Salad (recipe on facing page). A bright, bold blend of jicama, pineapple, and sweet potatoes is spooned atop fresh pineapple wheels for a memorable side dish.

Breads

If you've long thought of breads as so much unnecessary starch, think again: from bread sticks to muffins to moist pumpkin loaves, the recipes in this chapter fit right into your healthful eating plan. Moderate-size servings of these breads provide energy from complex carbohydrates without empty calories; they're low in fat and cholesterol, and they offer a satisfying source of B vitamins, iron, and fiber. So enjoy—just avoid high-fat spreads.

Pictured on page 82
Whole-grain Herb-Cheese Muffins

Per muffin:

143 calories (27% fat, 59% carbohydrates, 14% protein), 4 g total fat, 1 g saturated fat, 22 mg cholesterol, 21 g carbohydrates, 5 g protein, 157 mg sodium

Preparation time: About 15 minutes

Baking time: About 20 minutes

Move over croissants: make room for moist muffins! They're just the way to start the day (great at lunch and dinner, too).

- 2 tablespoons salad oil
- 1 large onion, minced
- 1 large green bell pepper, seeded and chopped
- 2 tablespoons honey
- 1 tablespoon Dijon mustard
- 1 cup nonfat milk
- 1 egg
- 2 egg whites
- 6 tablespoons shredded Cheddar cheese
- 1 cup whole wheat flour
- ½ cup *each* all-purpose flour and yellow cornmeal
- 2 teaspoons baking powder
- 1 teaspoon dry thyme leaves
- ⅛ teaspoon ground red pepper (cayenne)

Heat 1 tablespoon of the oil in a wide frying pan over medium heat. Add onion and bell pepper; cook, stirring often, until soft (about 10 minutes). Let cool.

In a large bowl, mix remaining 1 tablespoon oil, honey, mustard, milk, egg, egg whites, and ¼ cup of the cheese; then stir in onion mixture. In another bowl, stir together whole wheat flour, all-purpose flour, cornmeal, baking powder, thyme, and red pepper. Add egg mixture; stir just until evenly moistened. Spoon into 12 greased or paper-lined 2½-inch muffin cups, filling each about ⅔ full. Sprinkle with remaining 2 tablespoons cheese.

Bake in a 375° oven until muffins are well browned on top and a wooden pick inserted in center comes out clean (about 20 minutes). Makes 1 dozen muffins.

Pictured on page 74
Marjoram Scones

Per scone:

209 calories (27% fat, 64% carbohydrates, 9% protein), 6 g total fat, 1 g saturated fat, 1 mg cholesterol, 34 g carbohydrates, 5 g protein, 387 mg sodium

Preparation time: About 10 minutes

Baking time: About 25 minutes

The British call our cookies "biscuits"; their version of our biscuit is a "scone." By any name, these currant-flecked whole wheat triangles are delightful.

- About 1½ cups all-purpose flour
- ½ cup whole wheat flour
- ½ teaspoon *each* salt and baking soda
- 1 teaspoon dry marjoram leaves
- 2 teaspoons baking powder
- 2 tablespoons sugar
- ¼ cup margarine, cut into chunks
- ½ cup currants
- ¾ cup buttermilk

In a food processor or a large bowl, combine 1½ cups of the all-purpose flour, whole wheat flour, salt, baking soda, marjoram, baking powder, and sugar. Whirl or stir until well mixed. Add margarine; whirl or rub with your fingers until coarse crumbs form. Add currants; whirl or stir just until evenly distributed. Add buttermilk; whirl or stir just until dry ingredients are evenly moistened.

Lightly flour a board with all-purpose flour. Turn dough out onto a board and knead 12 turns. On a greased 12- by 15-inch baking sheet, pat dough evenly into a 6½-inch circle. With a knife, score dough to mark 8 equal wedges.

Bake scones in a 425° oven until well browned (about 25 minutes). Makes 8 scones.

*Sweet or savory? Breakfast is too early in the day for decision making,
so enjoy both: Date & Apricot Pumpkin Bread (recipe on facing page) and
Whole-grain Herb-Cheese Muffins (recipe on page 81).*

Pictured on facing page

Date & Apricot Pumpkin Bread

Preparation time: About 10 minutes

Baking time: About 1 hour

Studded with chopped dates and apricots, this spicy pumpkin bread is a special treat for family and friends.

- 1 egg
- 2 egg whites
- 1 cup *each* sugar and canned solid-pack pumpkin
- ⅓ cup salad oil
- ½ cup orange juice
- 2 cups all-purpose flour
- 1 teaspoon baking soda

Per serving:
248 calories (24% fat, 70% carbohydrates, 6% protein), 7 g total fat, .9 g saturated fat, 18 mg cholesterol, 44 g carbohydrates, 4 g protein, 103 mg sodium

- ½ teaspoon *each* baking powder and ground cinnamon, cloves, nutmeg, and ginger
- ½ cup *each* chopped dates and chopped dried apricots

In a large bowl, beat together egg, egg whites, sugar, pumpkin, oil, and orange juice.

In another bowl, stir together flour, baking soda, baking powder, cinnamon, cloves, nutmeg, and ginger; add to egg mixture and beat to blend. Stir in dates and apricots. Pour into a lightly greased 5- by 9-inch loaf pan.

Bake in a 350° oven until a wooden pick inserted in center of loaf comes out clean (about 1 hour). Let cool for 15 minutes; turn out onto a rack. Serve warm or cooled. Makes 1 loaf (10 to 12 servings).

Pictured on page 15

Raisin Pumpernickel Bread

Preparation time: About 15 minutes, plus 1½ hours to rise

Baking time: About 30 minutes

This dark, dense loaf gets its color and intense flavor from molasses, cocoa, and coffee. It's delicious at breakfast or with soup at supper.

- 2 packages active dry yeast
- 1¼ cups warm water (about 110°F)
- 1 cup *each* rye flour and whole wheat flour
- ¼ cup dark molasses
- 2 tablespoons unsweetened cocoa
- 1 tablespoon instant coffee powder
- ½ teaspoon salt
  About 1 cup all-purpose flour
- ½ cup raisins
  Cornmeal
- 1 egg white
- 1 tablespoon water

In a large bowl, combine yeast and the 1¼ cups warm water; let stand until softened (about 5 minutes). Add rye flour, whole wheat flour, molasses, cocoa, coffee powder, and salt. With a heavy spoon or dough hook, beat until flour is moistened.

Per serving:
142 calories (4% fat, 84% carbohydrates, 12% protein), 1 g total fat, .1 g saturated fat, 0 mg cholesterol, 31 g carbohydrates, 4 g protein, 104 mg sodium

If mixing by hand, stir in 1 cup of the all-purpose flour with a heavy spoon. Then scrape dough onto a floured board and knead until smooth and elastic (about 5 minutes), adding more all-purpose flour as needed to prevent sticking. *If using a dough hook*, mix in 1 cup of the all-purpose flour. Beat at medium speed until dough is smooth and elastic (about 3 minutes), adding more all-purpose flour as needed to prevent sticking.

Add raisins; knead until well distributed.

Place dough in an oiled bowl and turn over to grease top. Cover and let rise in a warm place until almost doubled in bulk (about 1 hour).

Sprinkle cornmeal in the center of a 12- by 15-inch baking sheet; set aside. Punch down dough, turn out onto a lightly floured board, and knead briefly to release air. Shape into a ball; place on cornmeal and press to form a 6-inch round. Cover lightly; let rise in a warm place until puffy (about 30 minutes).

Beat together egg white and the 1 tablespoon water; lightly brush over loaf. Bake in a 350° oven until loaf is a rich dark brown (about 30 minutes). Transfer to a rack. Serve warm or cooled. Makes 1 loaf (10 to 12 servings).

Bountiful Breakfasts

Blueberry Whole Wheat Pancakes

Fresh blueberries make these pancakes a sweet morning treat. They're marvelous plain, but you can top them with powdered sugar or your favorite syrup if you like.

- ¾ cup *each* all-purpose flour and whole wheat flour
- 2 teaspoons baking powder
- 4 teaspoons sugar
- 2 egg whites
- 1¼ cups nonfat milk
- 1½ tablespoons salad oil
- ¼ cup blueberries

In a small bowl, stir together all-purpose flour, whole wheat flour, baking powder, and sugar. Set aside.

In a large bowl, combine egg whites, milk, and oil. Add flour mixture and stir until just moistened; mixture will be lumpy. Stir in blueberries.

Heat a 12- to 14-inch nonstick frying pan over medium heat. For each cake, spoon about 3 tablespoons of batter into hot pan; spread to make a 4-inch circle. (You can cook about 4 pancakes at a time.) Cook until pancakes are bubbly on top (about 3 minutes); turn and cook until browned on bottom (about 2 more minutes). Makes 4 servings (about 16 pancakes).

■

Per serving: 263 calories (20% fat, 65% carbohydrates, 15% protein), 6 g total fat, .7 g saturated fat, 2 mg cholesterol, 43 g carbohydrates, 10 g protein, 280 mg sodium

Pancakes, sausages, eggs, and potatoes—mere memories of now-forbidden feasts? Not if you start your day with our suggestions: herbed turkey sausage, whole wheat griddlecakes dotted with blueberries, an egg-and-pepper scramble, and golden potato wedges. If you'd rather begin the morning with something sweetly simple, try our trifle; you can make it the night before. And for breakfast-time sipping, sample our fresh peach smoothie.

■

Spicy Sausage

Have turkey breast ground for you at the market; packaged ground turkey may contain skin and dark meat.

- 1 pound ground skinned turkey breast
- 1 teaspoon chopped fresh rosemary
- 2 teaspoons chopped fresh sage
- ½ teaspoon freshly ground pepper

In a large bowl, combine turkey, rosemary, sage, and pepper. Form mixture into 8 patties, each 3 inches wide and ¼ inch thick; place patties in a 12- to 14-inch frying pan (preferably nonstick). Cook over high heat for 1 minute; turn patties over and continue to cook for 1 more minute. Reduce heat; continue to cook, turning occasionally, until golden brown and cooked through (about 3 more minutes). Makes 4 servings.

■

Per serving: 133 calories (18% fat, 1% carbohydrates, 81% protein), 3 g total fat, .8 g saturated fat, 59 mg cholesterol, 0 g carbohydrates, 25 g protein, 58 mg sodium

Peppers & Eggs

Egg dishes without egg yolks? Perfectly possible and positively delicious, as this colorful scramble demonstrates.

- 1 teaspoon olive oil
- 1 medium-size onion, thinly sliced
- 1 *each* small green, red, and yellow bell pepper, seeded and very thinly sliced
- 8 egg whites, lightly beaten
- 2 tablespoons evaporated skim milk
- ¼ cup chopped parsley
- 1 tablespoon grated Parmesan cheese

Heat oil in a 10-inch frying pan (preferably nonstick) over medium-high heat. Add onion and cook, stirring, until slightly softened (about 5 minutes). Add bell peppers and cook, stirring, for 1 minute. Then cover and continue to cook until peppers are soft (about 2 more minutes).

Meanwhile, in a large bowl, beat together egg whites, milk, and parsley. Pour over pepper mixture; sprinkle with cheese, reduce heat to medium, cover, and cook until egg mixture is slightly firm and cheese is melted (about 2 minutes). Makes 4 servings.

■

Per serving: 74 calories (22% fat, 30% carbohydrates, 48% protein), 2 g total fat, .4 g saturated fat, 1 mg cholesterol, 6 g carbohydrates, 9 g protein, 145 mg sodium

Oven-baked Hash Browns

One taste of these baked potato wedges, and you'll forget fried potatoes forevermore. Just season the unpeeled potatoes with a little oil, paprika, and pepper, then slip them into a very hot oven until crisp and golden.

    1 teaspoon paprika
    ½ teaspoon pepper
    ¼ teaspoon salt (optional)
    1 tablespoon salad oil
    1½ pounds russet potatoes, unpeeled, cut into ½-inch-thick wedges

In a small bowl, combine paprika, pepper, and salt (if used). Lightly brush each of 2 baking sheets (preferably nonstick) with ½ teaspoon of the oil. Arrange potatoes on baking sheets, brush with 1 teaspoon more oil, and sprinkle with half the paprika mixture.

Bake in a 450° oven for about 15 minutes; turn, brush with remaining 1 teaspoon oil, and sprinkle with remaining paprika mixture. Continue to bake until potatoes are golden brown (about 10 more minutes). Makes 4 servings.

■

Per serving: 170 calories (20% fat, 72% carbohydrates, 8% protein), 4 g total fat, .4 g saturated fat, 0 mg cholesterol, 31 g carbohydrates, 3 g protein, 13 mg sodium

Yogurt Breakfast Trifle

This simple trifle looks impressive and goes together in a snap: just layer ladyfingers, strawberries, and orange yogurt. If you want, prepare the trifle ahead and chill it overnight.

     8 cups whole unhulled strawberries
    1½ tablespoons sugar
     ¾ cup orange juice
    24 Ladyfingers (page 96)
     3 cups lowfat orange yogurt

Reserve 6 of the prettiest strawberries. Hull and thinly slice remaining berries; mix with sugar and orange juice.

In each of 6 deep 2-cup bowls, place an even layer of Ladyfingers; cut and piece together, if needed. Spoon about ½ cup of the strawberry and juice mixture over Ladyfingers, then top with ¼ cup of the yogurt. Repeat layers. Garnish each trifle with a whole berry. Serve at once or cover and refrigerate for up to 1 day. Makes 6 servings.

■

Per serving: 344 calories (9% fat, 79% carbohydrates, 12% protein), 4 g total fat, 1 g saturated fat, 78 mg cholesterol, 70 g carbohydrates, 10 g protein, 118 mg sodium

Peach Smoothie

Blend buttermilk with frozen cubed peaches for a cool wake-up drink with a thick, slushy texture.

    3 large peaches (about 1 lb. *total*), peeled and pitted
      Lemon juice
    ⅓ cup buttermilk
    2 to 4 teaspoons sugar
      Fresh mint sprigs (optional)

Cut peaches into about ¾-inch chunks (you should have 1½ to 2 cups). Dip in lemon juice to coat, then set slightly apart in a single layer in a shallow pan. Cover and freeze until solid (about 2 hours). With a wide spatula, slide fruit from pan into plastic bags or freezer containers; return to freezer until ready to use.

To prepare smoothie, use 1½ cups of the frozen peaches. Let peaches stand at room temperature until slightly softened (about 5 minutes). Pour buttermilk into a blender or food processor. With motor running, add peach cubes, a few at a time (keep top of blender covered to prevent splashing); whirl until mixture is slushy. Blend in sugar.

Pour smoothie into a glass; top with mint sprigs, if desired. Serve at once. Makes 1 serving.

■

Per serving: 215 calories (4% fat, 87% carbohydrates, 9% protein), 1 g total fat, .5 g saturated fat, 3 mg cholesterol, 51 g carbohydrates, 5 g protein, 87 mg sodium

Pictured on facing page

No-Sauce Pizza

Per serving:

195 **calories** *(21% fat, 66% carbohydrates, 13% protein),*
4 g **total fat**, *1 g* **saturated fat**, *3 mg* **cholesterol**,
32 g **carbohydrates**, *7 g* **protein**, *362 mg* **sodium**

*Preparation time: About 20 minutes, plus 30 minutes to cook
onions and 2 hours to rise*

Baking time: About 20 minutes

This pizza isn't really missing anything. Slowly
simmered onions replace the traditional sauce;
tomatoes, oregano, and cheese go on top.

- 1 **package active dry yeast**
- ¾ **cup warm water (about 110°F)**
- 1 **teaspoon** *each* **sugar and salt**
  About 2 cups all-purpose flour
- 1½ **tablespoons olive oil**
- 3 **large onions, thinly sliced**
- 2 **pear-shaped (Roma-type) tomatoes**
  (about ⅓ lb. *total***), thinly sliced**
- ¼ **cup grated Parmesan cheese**
- 1 **tablespoon dry oregano leaves or**
  2 tablespoons fresh oregano leaves

If mixing by hand, stir in 1 cup more flour with a
heavy spoon. Scrape dough onto a lightly floured
board and knead until smooth and elastic (about 5
minutes), adding more flour as needed to prevent
sticking. *If using a dough hook*, mix in 1 cup more
flour. Beat at medium speed until dough is smooth
and elastic (about 3 minutes), adding more flour as
needed to prevent sticking.

Place dough in an oiled bowl and turn over to
grease top. Cover and let rise in a warm place until
doubled in bulk (about 2 hours).

Meanwhile, in a 12- to 14-inch frying pan, heat
1 tablespoon of the oil over medium-low heat.
Add onions and cook, stirring occasionally, until
soft and golden (about 30 minutes). Let cool.

Punch down dough and roll out to a 15-inch circle. Transfer to a lightly greased 14-inch pizza pan;
roll edge up and over to form a rim. Cover dough
with onions; layer on tomatoes, cheese, and oregano. Brush crust with remaining 1½ teaspoons oil.

Bake in a 425° oven until crust is golden (about
20 minutes). Serve hot. Makes 8 servings.

Pictured on front cover

Chewy Bread Sticks

Per bread stick:

99 **calories** *(14% fat, 73% carbohydrates, 13% protein),*
2 g **total fat**, *.2 g* **saturated fat**, *0 mg* **cholesterol**,
19 g **carbohydrates**, *3 g* **protein**, *98 mg* **sodium**

Preparation time: About 20 minutes, plus 15 minutes to rise

Baking time: About 15 minutes

These can be made in a jiffy—almost as quickly as
they'll be eaten!

- 1 **package active dry yeast**
- 1½ **cups warm water (about 110°F)**
- 1 **tablespoon honey**
- 1 **teaspoon salt**
- 3 **cups whole wheat flour**
  About 1¾ cups all-purpose flour
- 1 **tablespoon margarine, melted**
- ¼ **cup sesame seeds**

In a large bowl, combine yeast and warm water; let
stand until softened (about 5 minutes). Add honey,
salt, and whole wheat flour. With a heavy spoon or
dough hook, beat until flour is moistened.

If mixing by hand, stir in 1¾ cups of the all-
purpose flour with a heavy spoon. Scrape dough
onto a lightly floured board and knead until
smooth and elastic (about 10 minutes), adding more
all-purpose flour as needed to prevent sticking. *If
using a dough hook*, mix in 1¾ cups of the all-purpose
flour. Beat at medium speed until dough is smooth
and elastic (about 5 minutes), adding more all-
purpose flour as needed to prevent sticking.

Cut dough into 24 equal pieces. Roll each into
a 10-inch rope; place ropes 1 inch apart on lightly
greased 12- by 15-inch baking sheets. Let rise in a
warm place until slightly puffy (about 15 minutes).

Brush each rope lightly with margarine, then
sprinkle with sesame seeds. Bake in a 400° oven
until golden (about 15 minutes). Transfer to racks;
let cool slightly. Makes 2 dozen bread sticks.

You'll be too busy eating to miss the tomato sauce. Sweet sautéed onions,
sliced fresh tomatoes, and fresh oregano leaves top this crisp, thin-crusted
No-Sauce Pizza (recipe on facing page).

87

Desserts

Plain fresh fruit is one dessert that's always in favor with the

nutrition-conscious. Sometimes, though, we all crave

something a little richer and fancier—and not even the

juiciest berries or the most perfect ripe peach will do. When

you're in the mood for a dressed-up dessert, turn to this

chapter: you'll find cookies, cakes, puddings, and all manner

of fruit delights. And every one is low in fat, low in

cholesterol, and tops in sweetly satisfying taste. (For a

marvelous low-cholesterol brownie, see page 53.)

Creamy Chocolate Roll

Per serving:
*199 **calories** (17% fat, 70% carbohydrates, 13% protein),*
*4 g **total fat**, 2 g **saturated fat**, 30 mg **cholesterol**,*
*35 g **carbohydrates**, 7 g **protein**, 147 mg **sodium***

Preparation time: About 30 minutes

Baking time: About 10 minutes

Chilling time: At least 2 hours

You'd never guess this rich cake roll was made without chocolate bars and whipping cream!

- ¾ **cup all-purpose flour**
- ¼ **cup unsweetened cocoa**
- 1 **teaspoon baking powder**
- ¼ **teaspoon salt**
- 1 **egg**
- 1 **cup granulated sugar**
- ⅓ **cup water**
- 1 **teaspoon vanilla**
- 3 **egg whites**
- ½ **cup powdered sugar**
  Ricotta Filling (recipe follows)

Lightly grease a rimmed 10- by 15-inch baking pan and line it with wax paper; grease paper. In a bowl, mix flour, cocoa, baking powder, and salt.

In large bowl of an electric mixer, beat egg at high speed until thick and lemon-colored. Gradu-ally add granulated sugar; continue to beat, scraping bowl often, until mixture is creamy and pale. Beat in water and vanilla. Fold in flour mixture.

In small bowl of mixer, using clean, dry beaters, beat egg whites until they hold stiff peaks. Fold into batter. Pour into prepared pan; spread evenly.

Bake in a 375° oven until top of cake springs back when lightly pressed (about 10 minutes). Immediately invert cake onto a dishtowel sprinkled with 3 tablespoons of the powdered sugar. Peel off wax paper; immediately roll cake and towel into a cylinder, starting with a short side. Let cool completely on a rack. Meanwhile, prepare filling.

Unroll cooled cake, spread with filling, and reroll (do not be concerned if cake cracks). Wrap filled cake in plastic wrap and refrigerate for at least 2 hours or up to 24 hours. Sift remaining powdered sugar over cake before serving. Makes 12 servings.

Ricotta Filling. In small bowl of an electric mixer, combine 1 pound (about 2 cups) **part-skim ricotta cheese**, 3 tablespoons **powdered sugar**, ¼ cup finely chopped **candied orange peel**, and ½ teaspoon **almond extract.** Beat until well blended.

Angel Food Cake

Per serving:
*127 **calories** (.5% fat, 87% carbohydrates, 12.5% protein),*
*.1 g **total fat**, 0 g **saturated fat**, 0 mg **cholesterol**,*
*28 g **carbohydrates**, 4 g **protein**, 142 mg **sodium***

Preparation time: About 20 minutes

Baking time: 30 to 35 minutes

Airy, sweet, and snowy white—one taste tells you why angel food cake has been a favorite for so long.

- 1 **cup sifted cake flour**
- 1¼ **cups sugar**
- 12 **egg whites**
- ½ **teaspoon salt**
- 2 **teaspoons cream of tartar**
- 1½ **teaspoons vanilla or almond extract**

Sift together flour and ½ cup of the sugar; sift again and set aside.

In large bowl of an electric mixer, beat egg whites until foamy. Add salt and cream of tartar and continue to beat until mixture holds soft peaks. Add remaining ¾ cup sugar, 2 tablespoons at a time, beating well after each addition; continue to beat until mixture holds stiff peaks.

With a rubber spatula, fold in vanilla. Then sprinkle in flour mixture, about ¼ cup at a time, gently folding in each addition just until blended. Scrape batter into an ungreased 10-inch tube pan with a removable bottom; gently smooth top of batter. Slide spatula into batter and run it around pan to eliminate large air bubbles.

Bake in a 375° oven until cake is golden and springs back when lightly pressed (30 to 35 minutes). Invert pan on a funnel or pop bottle to keep cake from shrinking and falling. Let cake cool completely; remove from pan. Makes 12 servings.

Company will get comfortable with hot coffee and a cool dessert: Orange Pudding Parfaits (recipe on facing page). Simply alternate tapioca pudding and fresh orange segments in parfait glasses; top with Whipped Topping (page 76) and shredded orange peel, if you like.

Carrot Cake

Per serving:
216 *calories* (28% fat, 67% carbohydrates, 5% protein),
7 g *total fat*, .9 g *saturated fat*, 0 mg *cholesterol*,
37 g *carbohydrates*, 3 g *protein*, 173 mg *sodium*

Preparation time: About 20 minutes

Baking time: About 45 minutes

Crushed pineapple, golden raisins, and plenty of shredded carrots give this hearty cake an appealing texture. A simple glaze made with pineapple juice replaces the traditional cream cheese frosting.

    1 cup *each* all-purpose flour and
      whole wheat flour
 1½ tablespoons ground cinnamon
    1 teaspoon ground nutmeg
    2 teaspoons *each* baking soda and
      baking powder
   ½ teaspoon salt
    1 cup firmly packed brown sugar
   ½ cup granulated sugar
    1 can (about 8 oz.) crushed pineapple
      packed in its own juice
   ¾ cup salad oil
    6 egg whites
    1 teaspoon vanilla
    3 cups finely shredded carrots
 1½ cups golden raisins
      Pineapple Glaze (recipe follows)

In a large bowl, stir together all-purpose flour, whole wheat flour, cinnamon, nutmeg, baking soda, baking powder, salt, brown sugar, and granulated sugar. Set aside.

Drain pineapple, reserving juice for glaze. Place pineapple, oil, egg whites, vanilla, and carrots in large bowl of an electric mixer; beat until well combined. Add pineapple mixture and raisins to flour mixture; stir until evenly moistened. Spoon into a well-greased, flour-dusted 9- by 13-inch baking pan.

Bake in a 350° oven until a wooden pick inserted in center of cake comes out clean (about 45 minutes). Let cool in pan on a rack. Prepare Pineapple Glaze and pour over cake. To serve, cut into about 2- by 2¼-inch squares. Makes 24 servings.

Pineapple Glaze. Mix 1½ cups sifted **powdered sugar** and about ¼ cup of the **reserved pineapple juice** until mixture is smoothly blended and has a good pouring consistency.

Pictured on facing page

Orange Pudding Parfaits

Per serving:
189 *calories* (2% fat, 82% carbohydrates, 16% protein),
.4 g *total fat*, .2 g *saturated fat*, 3 mg *cholesterol*,
40 g *carbohydrates*, 8 g *protein*, 105 mg *sodium*

Preparation time: About 30 minutes

Cooking time: About 7 minutes

Chilling time: About 4 hours

Layers of fresh orange segments and tapioca pudding add up to a picture-perfect dessert.

    3 tablespoons quick-cooking tapioca
   ⅓ cup sugar
    2 egg whites
 2½ cups nonfat milk
   ½ teaspoon vanilla
    1 tablespoon *each* grated orange peel and
      orange-flavored liqueur
    2 large oranges

In a 2- to 3-quart pan, stir together tapioca, sugar, egg whites, and milk; let stand for 5 minutes. Then bring to a full boil over medium heat, stirring constantly. Remove from heat and stir in vanilla, orange peel, and liqueur. Let cool, uncovered, stirring once after 20 minutes.

Using a sharp knife, cut peel and all white membrane from oranges; cut segments free and lift out. Layer cooled tapioca and orange segments in four 8-ounce parfait glasses. Cover and refrigerate until cold before serving (about 4 hours). Makes 4 servings.

Strawberry Cream

Per serving:

*190 **calories** (25% fat, 54% carbohydrates, 21% protein),
5 g **total fat**, 3 g **saturated fat**, 20 mg **cholesterol**,
26 g **carbohydrates**, 10 g **protein**, 108 mg **sodium***

Preparation time: About 45 minutes

Chilling time: At least 4 hours

This sweet, cold treat serves up a double dose of strawberries, blending the fresh fruit with flavored yogurt. Serve it in clear dessert glasses to show off the pretty layers of pink berry cream and deep red strawberry purée.

Strawberry Purée (recipe follows)
2 **cups sliced hulled strawberries**
½ **cup sugar**
1 **envelope unflavored gelatin**
¾ **cup cold water**
2 **egg whites**
2 **cups (about 1 lb.) part-skim ricotta cheese**
1 **cup lowfat strawberry yogurt**
8 **whole unhulled strawberries**

Prepare Strawberry Purée; refrigerate. Meanwhile, place sliced strawberries and sugar in a bowl. Partially crush berries with a fork or potato masher (there should still be some berry chunks); set aside.

In a 1-quart pan, sprinkle gelatin over cold water and let stand for about 5 minutes to soften. Stir in berry-sugar mixture. Bring just to a boil, stirring constantly; then pour into a large bowl and let cool until thick but not set (about 20 minutes).

In small bowl of an electric mixer, beat egg whites until they hold stiff peaks. Fold into berry mixture. Beat ricotta cheese and yogurt with mixer until blended; fold into berry mixture.

Divide mixture equally among eight 8-ounce dessert glasses. Cover and refrigerate until set (at least 4 hours) or until next day. To serve, pour Strawberry Purée equally into dessert glasses; top each serving with a whole strawberry. Makes 8 servings.

Strawberry Purée. In a blender or food processor, whirl 1 cup hulled **strawberries** until puréed. Sweeten purée with about 1 tablespoon **powdered sugar** (or to taste). Cover and refrigerate for at least 4 hours or up to 1 day.

Rice Pudding

Per serving:

*117 **calories** (2% fat, 81% carbohydrates, 17% protein),
.3 g **total fat**, .2 g **saturated fat**, 2 mg **cholesterol**,
23 g **carbohydrates**, 5 g **protein**, 64 mg **sodium***

Preparation time: About 5 minutes

Baking time: About 3 hours

Simple, and simply superb! Rice pudding is "comfort food," certain to bring back happy memories (or begin delightful new traditions).

3 **cups nonfat milk**
⅓ **cup short-grain rice, such as pearl**
¼ **cup sugar**
½ **teaspoon vanilla**
¼ **teaspoon ground nutmeg**

In a 9-inch square baking dish or a shallow 2- to 3-quart casserole, combine milk, rice, sugar, vanilla, and nutmeg. Cover and bake in a 300° oven until thick and light golden in color (about 3 hours). Or bake pudding uncovered; an amber, caramel-flavored skin will form on top. Serve pudding warm. Makes 4 to 6 servings.

Orange-Apple Strudel

Per serving:

175 calories (13% fat, 84% carbohydrates, 3% protein), 3 g total fat, .4 g saturated fat, 0 mg cholesterol, 38 g carbohydrates, 1 g protein, 60 mg sodium

Preparation time: About 45 minutes

Baking time: About 45 minutes

Layers of crisp, delicate fila pastry enclose a spicy apple filling accented with orange peel.

> 2 **pounds tart green-skinned apples, such as Granny Smith**
> 2 **teaspoons grated orange peel**
> ½ **cup firmly packed brown sugar**
> ¼ **cup all-purpose flour**
> 1 **teaspoon ground cinnamon**
> ½ **teaspoon ground nutmeg**
> 3 **sheets fila pastry, thawed if frozen**
> 2 **tablespoons margarine, melted**
> **Orange Sauce (recipe follows)**

Peel and core apples, then thinly slice them into a large bowl. Mix in orange peel, sugar, flour, cinnamon, and nutmeg.

Lay one sheet of fila pastry on a baking sheet. With a pastry brush, lightly brush fila with 1½ teaspoons of the margarine. Stack remaining 2 fila sheets on top, brushing each with 1½ teaspoons margarine. Then spoon apple mixture in a strip down one long side of stacked fila sheets, 1½ inches in from side and extending to about 1 inch from ends. Fold ends of fila over filling, then roll up fila jelly roll style, starting at side nearest filling. Brush with remaining 1½ teaspoons margarine.

Bake in a 375° oven until pastry is rich golden brown (about 45 minutes). Meanwhile, prepare Orange Sauce. Let strudel cool on baking sheet on a rack. Serve warm or at room temperature.

To serve, cut crosswise; pour 2 tablespoons Orange Sauce over slices. Makes 10 servings.

Orange Sauce. In a 1- to 2-quart pan, stir together 1 tablespoon *each* **cornstarch** and **water.** Add 1 cup **orange juice** and ¼ cup **orange marmalade.** Bring to a boil over high heat, stirring. Serve hot or at room temperature. If made ahead, cover and refrigerate until next day; before serving, bring to room temperature or stir over medium-high heat until hot (about 2 minutes).

Baked Pineapple Compote

Per serving:

266 calories (3% fat, 82% carbohydrates, 15% protein), 5 g total fat, .7 g saturated fat, 0 mg cholesterol, 60 g carbohydrates, 2 g protein, 52 mg sodium

Preparation time: About 20 minutes

Cooking time: About 20 minutes

Toss pineapple chunks, prunes, and raspberries with a tart-sweet brown sugar sauce, then present the mixture in hollowed-out pineapple shells.

> 1 **large pineapple (about 5 lbs.)**
> 8 **ounces pitted prunes (about 1⅓ cups)**
> ¼ **cup firmly packed brown sugar**
> 2 **tablespoons margarine**
> 2 **tablespoons lemon juice**
> 1 **cup fresh or thawed frozen unsweetened raspberries**

Cut pineapple in half lengthwise through crown. Next, cut around edge of each half with a grape-fruit knife, cutting about ¾ inch in from edge. Cut out and discard core from each half. Cut fruit (still in shells) crosswise, then lengthwise to make 1- to 1½-inch chunks. Slide knife beneath chunks to free them from shells; remove chunks and set aside. Pour pineapple juice out of shells into a 2- to 3-quart pan and set aside.

Return pineapple chunks to shells. Place shells, cut side up, in a rimmed 12- by 15-inch baking pan. Bake in a 400° oven until pineapple chunks are hot to the touch (about 15 minutes).

Meanwhile, stir prunes, sugar, and margarine into pineapple juice in pan; bring to a boil over high heat. Reduce heat, cover, and simmer, stirring occasionally, until sauce is slightly thickened (about 15 minutes). Mix in lemon juice. Spoon prune mixture evenly over warm pineapple chunks in shells; mix gently, then top with raspberries.

To serve, place shells on a platter; then spoon fruit into individual bowls. Makes 6 servings.

Raspberries in Meringue

Per serving:

151 **calories** *(2% fat, 92% carbohydrates, 6% protein),*
.4 g **total fat**, *0 g* **saturated fat**, *0 mg* **cholesterol**,
36 g **carbohydrates**, *2 g* **protein**, *25 mg* **sodium**

Preparation time: About 1 hour, plus at least 4 hours to chill Raspberry Purée and 3 to 4 hours to dry meringues

Baking time: 1 hour

Just right for a special occasion are these delicate meringue shells filled with juicy fresh raspberries and crowned with sweetened raspberry purée.

> **Raspberry Purée (recipe follows)**
> 4 **egg whites**
> ½ **teaspoon cream of tartar**
> 1 **cup sugar**
> 1 **teaspoon vanilla**
> 2 **cups raspberries**

Prepare Raspberry Purée; refrigerate. Cover a large baking sheet with ungreased plain brown or parchment paper. Trace eight 3½-inch circles on paper, spacing 1½ inches apart.

In large bowl of an electric mixer, combine egg whites and cream of tartar. Beat on high speed until foamy. Gradually add sugar, about 1 tablespoon at a time; continue to beat, scraping sides of bowl often, until mixture holds stiff, glossy peaks. Fold in vanilla.

Spoon about ½ cup of the meringue onto each circle on prepared baking sheet. Using back of spoon, spread mixture to cover each circle; then build up a 1½-inch-high rim, creating a hollow in each shell. (Or spoon mixture into a pastry bag fitted with a large star tip; pipe onto traced circles, building up a rim as directed.) Position baking sheet just below center of a 250° oven. Bake for 1 hour; turn off heat and leave meringues in closed oven until dry to the touch (3 to 4 hours).

Remove baking sheet from oven. Let meringues cool completely on baking sheet on a rack; then carefully peel off paper backing. If made ahead, store in an airtight container for up to 5 days.

To serve, fill meringue shells with raspberries; pour an eighth of the Raspberry Purée over each serving. Makes 8 servings.

Raspberry Purée. In a blender or food processor, whirl 3 cups **raspberries** until puréed. To remove seeds, push purée through a fine wire strainer set over a bowl. Sweeten purée with about 2 tablespoons **powdered sugar** (or to taste). Cover and refrigerate for at least 4 hours or up to 1 day.

Peach & Berry Bake

Per serving:

203 **calories** *(25% fat, 69% carbohydrates, 6% protein),*
6 g **total fat**, *1 g* **saturated fat**, *24 mg* **cholesterol**,
36 g **carbohydrates**, *3 g* **protein**, *117 mg* **sodium**

Preparation time: About 15 minutes

Baking time: About 45 minutes

Down-home delicious! This crumb-topped fruit casserole boasts the best of summer's bounty.

> 1 **tablespoon cornstarch**
> 1 **teaspoon ground cinnamon**
> ½ **teaspoon ground nutmeg**
> ½ **cup sugar**
> 4 **cups sliced peeled peaches (about 2 lbs.)**
> 1 **cup blueberries**
> 1 **cup all-purpose flour**
> 1 **teaspoon baking powder**
> ¼ **cup margarine**

> 1 **egg**
> ¾ **cup orange juice**
> 2 **tablespoons lemon juice**

In a shallow 1½- to 2-quart baking dish, mix cornstarch, cinnamon, nutmeg, and ¼ cup of the sugar. Stir in peaches and blueberries.

In a food processor or a bowl, combine flour, baking powder, remaining ¼ cup sugar, and margarine. Whirl (or rub with your fingers) until mixture has the texture of coarse cornmeal. Add egg; whirl or stir just until well blended. Sprinkle mixture evenly over fruit. In a small bowl, mix orange juice and lemon juice; pour evenly over crumbs.

Bake in a 375° oven until fruit mixture is bubbly in center and topping is golden (about 45 minutes). Serve warm or cooled. Makes 9 servings.

End an evening with an elegant dessert—mint-garnished
Raspberries in Meringue (recipe on facing page). To keep the meringue shells
crisp, don't make them on a humid day (they absorb moisture easily)
and fill them just before serving.

Poached Pears in Red Wine

Per serving:

262 calories (2% fat, 96% carbohydrates, 2% protein), 1 g total fat, 0 g saturated fat, 0 mg cholesterol, 67 g carbohydrates, 1 g protein, 9 mg sodium

Preparation time: About 15 minutes

Cooking time: About 50 minutes

Chilling time: At least 4 hours

Spice up a winter evening with tender poached pears. The sweetened red wine used as the poaching liquid doubles as a rich, fragrant sauce for the fruit.

> **4 cups water**
> **¼ cup orange juice**
> **4 medium-size firm-ripe pears, such as Bartlett or Bosc**
> **2 teaspoons grated orange peel**
> **¾ cup sugar**
> **3 cups dry red wine**
> **1 cinnamon stick (about 3 inches long)**

In a large bowl, combine water and 2 tablespoons of the orange juice. Then peel pears, leaving stems in place; remove core from each pear by inserting an apple corer through blossom end. As each pear is prepared, immediately immerse it in water-juice mixture.

In a 2-quart pan, combine remaining 2 tablespoons orange juice, orange peel, sugar, wine, and cinnamon stick. Bring to a boil; then reduce heat and simmer for 5 minutes. Drain pears and add them to wine mixture. Cover and simmer until pears are just tender when pierced (about 20 minutes).

With a slotted spoon, lift pears from liquid, arrange in a serving dish, and set aside. Increase heat to high, bring wine mixture to a boil, and boil until reduced to 1 cup (about 20 minutes). Discard cinnamon stick; then pour sauce over pears. Refrigerate until well chilled (at least 4 hours or up to 1 day), basting occasionally with sauce. Makes 4 servings.

Ladyfingers

Per ladyfinger:

35 calories (9% fat, 80% carbohydrates, 11% protein), .4 g total fat, .1 g saturated fat, 14 mg cholesterol, 7 g carbohydrates, 1 g protein, 12 mg sodium

Preparation time: About 45 minutes

Baking time: 9 to 10 minutes

These delicate little cakes are a simple, sweet companion for fruit compotes and creams.

> **Cornstarch**
> **¾ cup plus 1 tablespoon sifted all-purpose flour**
> **Dash of salt**
> **⅔ cup sugar**
> **2 eggs, separated**
> **2 egg whites**
> **1 teaspoon vanilla**

Grease 2 baking sheets, then dust with cornstarch. (Or use greased, cornstarch-dusted ladyfinger pans.) Set aside.

Sift flour with salt and ⅓ cup of the sugar; set aside.

In large bowl of an electric mixer, beat all 4 egg whites until they hold stiff peaks; then gradually beat in remaining ⅓ cup sugar, 1 tablespoon at a time. In small bowl of mixer, beat egg yolks with vanilla until thick and lemon-colored. Fold yolk mixture into egg white mixture. Sift flour mixture over egg mixture; carefully fold in.

Spoon batter into a pastry bag fitted with a plain tip. Pipe batter onto prepared baking sheets, forming about 1- by 4-inch fingers; space fingers about 1 inch apart. (Or spoon batter into ladyfinger pans.)

Bake in a 350° oven until lightly browned (9 to 10 minutes). Let cool on baking sheets (or in pans) on racks for about a minute, then transfer to racks and let cool completely. Store airtight. Makes 2½ dozen ladyfingers.

Pictured on page 47

Oatmeal Raisin Cookies

Per cookie:

81 calories (29% fat, 63% carbohydrates, 8% protein), 3 g total fat, .3 g saturated fat, 0 mg cholesterol, 13 g carbohydrates, 2 g protein, 23 mg sodium

Preparation time: About 15 minutes

Baking time: About 10 minutes

Spicy, cakelike cookies studded with golden raisins are sure to satisfy the cookie crowd. We've used both oat bran and rolled oats in the dough (look for oat bran in the cereal aisle of your supermarket).

- 1 **cup all-purpose flour**
- ½ **cup oat bran**
- ½ **teaspoon ground allspice**
- 1 **teaspoon baking soda**
- ½ **teaspoon salt (optional)**
- 1 **cup firmly packed brown sugar**
- ½ **cup salad oil**
- ½ **cup nonfat milk**
- 2 **egg whites**
- 1 **teaspoon vanilla**
- 3 **cups rolled oats**
- 1 **cup golden raisins**

In a small bowl, stir together flour, oat bran, allspice, baking soda, and salt (if desired) until well combined. Set aside.

In large bowl of an electric mixer, beat sugar and oil until creamy. Add milk, egg whites, and vanilla; beat until well combined. Gradually add flour mixture, beating until well blended. Stir in oats and raisins.

Drop rounded tablespoonfuls of dough about 2 inches apart on ungreased baking sheets. Bake in a 375° oven until cookies are light golden (about 10 minutes). Let cool on baking sheets on racks for about 2 minutes; then transfer cookies to racks and let cool completely. Store airtight. Makes 4 dozen cookies.

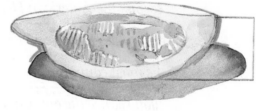

Lemon Ice

Per serving:

90 calories (.5% fat, 99% carbohydrates, .5% protein), .1 g total fat, 0 g saturated fat, 0 mg cholesterol, 24 g carbohydrates, .2 g protein, 18 mg sodium

Preparation time: 50 to 60 minutes

Freezing time: About 6 hours

On a sweltering summer night, treat yourself to the tangy, icy cold refreshment of lemon *granita*.

- 1 **small lemon**
  About ½ cup fresh lemon juice
- 1 **cup sugar**
- 4 **cups water**
  Dash of salt

Using a vegetable peeler or a sharp knife, cut peel (yellow part only) from lemon. Squeeze juice from lemon into a glass measure, then add enough additional fresh lemon juice (you'll need about ½ cup) to make ⅔ cup total. Cover juice and set aside.

Cut lemon peel into ½-inch pieces; place in a food processor along with sugar and whirl until peel is finely chopped. Pour mixture into a 3-quart pan, add water and salt, and heat, stirring, just until sugar is dissolved. Let cool; stir in lemon juice. Pour mixture into an 8- or 9-inch square metal pan, cover, and freeze until solid (about 4 hours).

Let ice stand at room temperature until you can break it into chunks with a heavy spoon. Whirl chunks, a portion at a time, in a food processor; use on-off pulses at first to break up chunks, then whirl continuously until smooth and slushy. (Or place all chunks in large bowl of an electric mixer; beat until smooth and slushy, increasing mixer speed from low to high as ice softens.)

Pour ice into a freezer container, cover airtight, and freeze until firm (about 2 hours). For best flavor and texture, serve ice within 2 months. To serve hard-frozen ice, let stand at room temperature until slightly softened before scooping. Makes 9 servings (about 4½ cups).

Appendix

The useful guides and references in this chapter will help you follow a healthful eating plan. You'll find a glossary of terms; the American Heart Association Diet, reprinted in full; tables that provide nutritional information on many of the most common foods; a list of substitutions that can help you reduce the amount of cholesterol and fat in your diet; and herbs and spices you can use to perk up your recipes. To guide your marketing, we also explain how to read package labels. At the end of the chapter, you'll find weight tables to help you determine the number of calories to eat each day.

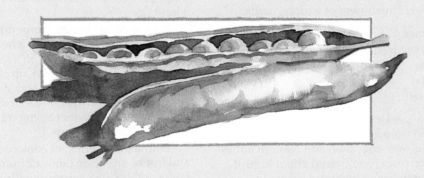

Glossary

Atherosclerosis. Process in which the lining of the arteries becomes coated with fatty substances. Blood vessels are narrowed and scarred by the deposits and may eventually become completely blocked. If the blockage occurs in an artery supplying blood to the heart, a heart attack results; if the blockage occurs in an artery that supplies blood to the brain, a stroke results.

Calorie. Measurement of the amount of energy produced when food is metabolized.

Carbohydrates. One of three major nutrients supplying energy to the body (the other two are fat and protein). Providing fiber and about 4 calories per gram, carbohydrates are our most efficient source of energy, more readily available for use by the body than protein or fat. They're essential for proper function of the brain and nervous system.

Carbohydrates are categorized as simple or complex. *Simple carbohydrates* are found in honey, syrups, jams, jellies, fruit, and fruit juices. *Complex carbohydrates*, classified as water soluble or water insoluble, are found in foods such as whole grains, breads, legumes, and most fruits and vegetables.

Cholesterol. A waxy, fatlike substance essential to the structure of cell membranes and nerve sheaths and the production of vitamins and hormones. Your liver manufactures sufficient cholesterol for the body's needs; *dietary cholesterol* comes from the foods you eat. Cholesterol is present in all foods of animal origin: meat, poultry, fish, eggs, and dairy products.

Both dietary cholesterol and the cholesterol your body makes affect the amount of cholesterol circulating in your bloodstream. That amount, measured in milligrams per deciliter, is known as your blood cholesterol level.

Fat. One of three major nutrients supplying energy to the body (the other two are carbohydrates and protein). Supplying about 9 calories per gram, fats play an important role in cell maintenance and vitamin absorption.

Fats are classified as saturated or unsaturated; unsaturated fats are further categorized as monounsaturated or polyunsaturated. *Saturated fats*, usually solid at room temperature, are typically found in foods of animal origin (such as meat and whole-milk dairy products) and in some vegetable products (palm and coconut oils, for example). Saturated fats tend to raise your blood cholesterol level.

Unsaturated fats, typically liquid at room temperature, most often come from plants and may help lower your blood cholesterol. *Monounsaturated fats* include olive, peanut, and avocado oils; among *polyunsaturated fats* are corn, safflower, and sesame oils.

Hydrogenated fats such as margarine and vegetable shortening are polyunsaturated oils that have been converted to a more saturated form through the addition of hydrogen (a commercial process called hydrogenation). These fats tend to raise blood cholesterol.

Omega-3 fatty acids, a group of polyunsaturated fats found primarily in coldwater marine fish such as salmon and tuna, may help lower your cholesterol level.

Dietary fiber. The undigested portion of food. Found only in plants, it is either water soluble or water insoluble. Some types of fiber may help to lower your blood cholesterol level; see "Fiber Fads," page 60.

Lipoproteins. Fat-protein molecules that carry cholesterol in the blood. *High-density lipoprotein* (HDL), known as good cholesterol, may be responsible for carrying cholesterol away from cells and tissues back to the liver for elimination. It's assumed to protect against atherosclerosis. *Low-density lipoprotein* (LDL), often termed bad cholesterol, may be responsible for depositing cholesterol on the artery walls. A higher LDL level is assumed to indicate greater risk of atherosclerosis.

Protein. One of three major nutrients supplying energy to the body (the other two are fat and carbohydrates). Protein provides about 4 calories per gram. It's made up of amino acids, substances essential to maintaining muscles, bone, skin, and blood. Animal products provide *complete protein*—protein that contains all eight of the amino acids required for good health. Plant products (except soybeans) provide *incomplete protein*, supplying less than the full range of essential amino acids. But by combining plant foods (by mixing grains with legumes, for example), you can usually correct such deficiencies.

The American Heart Association Diet

Vegetables & Fruits

High in Vitamins, Minerals, Potassium, Fiber; Low in Fat, Calories, Sodium…Contain *no* Cholesterol

Okay Foods:

Almost all vegetables and fruits are "Okay Foods" and should be part of your daily eating plan.

Use at least 3 servings (Sv) of fruit or real fruit juice every day. (1 Sv = 1 medium-sized piece of fruit or ½ cup juice or canned fruit.) Also, use at least 3 servings of vegetables every day. (1 Sv = ½ to 1 cup, cooked or raw.)

Include *at least one serving* from the High Vitamin C list every day and *at least one serving* from the High Vitamin A list several times a week:

High Vitamin C—Asparagus, broccoli, cabbage, cantaloupe, grapefruit, greens (mustard, beet, kale, collards), green pepper, oranges, potatoes, spinach, strawberries, tangerines, tomatoes.

High Vitamin A—Broccoli, cantaloupe, carrots, greens, peaches, pumpkin, spinach, sweet potatoes, winter squash.

When you are reducing your intake of red meat and egg yolks, you can *increase your iron intake* by eating more green, leafy vegetables; peas and beans (fresh and dried); dried fruits; and whole-grain or enriched cereals. *Your body can make better use of the iron these foods provide if you eat them along with a good source of Vitamin C.*

Enjoy plenty of vegetables and fruits. If you are watching your weight, these foods will give you the most nutrition for the fewest calories.

Foods to Avoid:

Almost all fruits and vegetables are very low in fat, except:

Coconut, Coconut Oil, Palm Oil, and Palm Kernel Oil—Contain saturated fat and should be avoided.

Olives ▲ *and Avocados*—Also contain fat (and therefore are higher in calories). Tips for using these are included in the "Fats and Oils" section.

Milk Products

High in Protein, Calcium, Phosphorus, Niacin, Riboflavin, Vitamins A and D

Okay Foods:

Milk Products Containing Only 0–1% Milk Fat—Skim milk or fluid nonfat milk *(0% fat)*; low-fat milk *(1% fat)*; nonfat or low-fat dry milk; evaporated skim milk; buttermilk made from skim or low-fat milk; skim or low-fat yogurt; drinks made with skim or low-fat milk and cocoa or other low-fat drink powders; ice milk, sherbet, frozen low-fat yogurt.

Low-Fat Cheeses—Dry-curd or low-fat cottage cheese ▲; low-fat natural cheeses ▲ or processed special cheeses ▲ *labeled as containing not more than two grams of fat per ounce.*

Begin trying lower-in-fat milk products. Whole milk is 4% fat. If you use whole milk now, first try 2% fat milk…Then move along to 1% fat milk…Soon, you will enjoy the taste of skim milk.

Look for milk products labeled *fortified with vitamins A and D*. Adults and young children need 2 servings daily (1 Sv = 8 oz. low-fat or skim milk or yogurt, 2 oz. low-fat cheese, or ½ cup low-fat cottage cheese); older children, teenagers and women who are pregnant or breastfeeding need 3–4 servings.

Foods to Avoid:

Milk Products Containing More Than 1% Milk Fat—Low-fat milk with 1½–2% milk fat; whole milk; dried whole milk; buttermilk or yogurt made from whole milk; drinks made from whole milk; condensed milk; evaporated milk; ice cream.

Cream, All Kinds—Half and half, light, heavy, whipping or sour.

Nondairy Cream Substitutes—Coffee creamers, sour cream substitutes made with *coconut, palm, or palm kernel oil, which are high in saturated fat.* Look for special ones labeled *"made from poly-unsaturated fat."*

All Cheeses Containing More Than 2 Grams of Fat Per Ounce—Cream cheese ■, creamed cottage cheese ■ and most other natural and processed cheeses ■ such as American, Swiss, mozzarella and blue.

Fats & Oils

Some of these foods are high in Vitamin A or E, but *all* are high in fat and calories. The amount of food per serving (Sv) is described for each item so you can keep track of fat intake in teaspoons (tsp).

Okay Foods:

Vegetable Oils—Safflower, sunflower, corn, partially hydrogenated soybean, cottonseed, sesame, canola, olive. (1 Sv = 1 tsp)

Margarines—Stick, tub, squeeze (1 Sv = 1 tsp) or diet (1 Sv = 2 tsp)—One of the "Okay" vegetable oils should be listed as the first ingredient on the label with twice as much polyunsaturated as saturated fat.

Salad Dressing and Mayonnaise ●— Homemade or store-bought, made with "Okay" oils (1 Sv = 2 tsp). Low-calorie dressings ● can be used as desired.

Seeds and Nuts—All seeds ● (pumpkin, sesame, sunflower) and most nuts ● (except cashew and macadamia). (1 Sv = 3 tsp)

Avocados and Olives ▲—Use only in small amounts. (1 Sv = 3 tsp chopped)

Peanut Butter ●—Count as a fat (1 Sv = 2 tsp) or use as a "Meatless Main Dish." (1 Sv = 3 tsp)

Peanut Oil—This choice is not as good as the "Okay" oils. It may be used sparingly for a flavor change.

Depending upon your need for weight control, use no more than 5–8 servings of "Okay" fats and oils per day.

Remember to count the "hidden fats" (in bakery products and snack foods, in cooking, on vegetables and breads).

Use cooking styles which use little or no fat—instead of frying, try roasting, broiling, steaming.

Foods to Avoid:

Solid Fats and Shortenings—Butter ●, bacon drippings ■, ham hocks ■, lard, salt pork ■, meat fat and drippings, gravy from meat drippings, shortening, suet; margarines except those listed as "Okay."

Chocolate, Coconut, Coconut Oil, Palm Oil, or Palm Kernel Oil—These are often used in bakery products, nondairy creamers, whipped toppings, candy and commercially fried foods. *Read labels carefully.*

Breads, Cereals, Pasta & Starchy Vegetables

Low in Fat and Cholesterol; High in B Vitamins, Iron, Fiber

Okay Foods:

Low-Fat Breads—All kinds (wheat, rye, raisin, white); those with whole-grain or enriched flours are best. (1 Sv = 1 slice)

Low-Fat Rolls—English muffins, frankfurter and hamburger buns, water (not egg) bagels, pita bread, tortillas (not fried).

Low-Fat Crackers and Snacks—Animal, graham, rye, saltine ●, oyster ● and matzo crackers; store-bought fig bar, ginger snap and molasses cookies; bread sticks, melba toast, rusks and flatbread; pretzels ●, popcorn ● (with "Okay" fat).

Hot or Cold Cereals—All kinds, except granola-type cereals with coconut or coconut oil. (1 Sv = ¼–¾ cup)

Rice and Pasta—All kinds (pasta made without egg). (1 Sv = ½ cup)

Starchy Vegetables—Potatoes, lima beans, green peas, winter squash, corn, yams or sweet potatoes. (1 Sv = ¼–½ cup)

Quick Breads—Home-made with "Okay" fats, oils and milk products—Biscuits, muffins, cornbread, banana bread, soft rolls, pancakes, French toast and waffles. Use your weekly egg yolk allowance (3 per week), or try egg whites in recipes. Use two egg whites instead of one whole egg.

Low-Fat Soups—Broth ●, bouillon ●, chicken noodle ●, tomato-based seafood chowders ●, minestrone ●, onion ●, split pea ●, tomato ●, vegetarian vegetable ● Use the canned or powdered varieties, but *read labels* to choose those lowest in salt and fat. Better still, make soups at home so that you can avoid salt, fat, cream, whole milk or cheese. (1 Sv = 1 cup)

Breads, cereals, pasta and starchy vegetables (in moderate-sized portions) are not extremely high in calories. It's the fat and sauces added to them that run up the total calories.

Stretch your meat allowance and your budget by combining small portions of poultry, fish or meat with vegetables, herbs, and rice or pasta.

Foods to Avoid:

Products made with egg yolks or with "AVOID" fats, oils and whole milk products:

Butter rolls, egg breads, egg bagels, cheese breads, croissants, commercial doughnuts, muffins, sweet rolls, biscuits, waffles, pancakes; buttered popcorn ■ store-bought mixes.

High-fat commercial crackers such as cheese crackers ■, butter crackers ■ and those made with coconut oil, palm oil, or palm kernel oil.

Pasta, rice and vegetables prepared with whole eggs, cream sauce or high-fat cheese; or fried in "AVOID" fats.

Cream soups ■, vichyssoise ■ and chunky-style soups ■ which have large amounts of meat in them.

Meat, Poultry, Seafood, Nuts...Dried Beans & Peas...Eggs

High in Protein, B Vitamins, Iron, Other Minerals

Okay Foods:

Chicken and Turkey—Trim the skin; this is where much of the fat is found.

Lean Beef, Veal, Pork, Lamb—Trim all visible fat.

Fish and Shellfish—All kinds, but limit the use of shrimp or lobster to *no more than* one serving of one of these per week.

Meatless or "Low-Meat" Main Dishes—Try recipes with dried beans, peas, lentils, soybean curd (tofu), peanut butter ● or low-fat cheese ▲ instead of meat a few times a week. Also try combining small amounts of meat, fish or poultry with rice or pasta in mixed dishes or casseroles.

Egg Whites—But limit whole eggs or egg yolks to no more than four per week.

Wild Game—Rabbit, pheasant, venison, wild duck and other wild game animals generally have less fat than animals raised for the market.

Adults need no more than 6 ounces of meat, poultry or seafood per day (about two small servings). Examples of a 3-ounce portion:
- ½ of a chicken breast or a chicken leg and a thigh together
- ½ cup of flaked fish
- 2 thin slices lean roast beef (3" x 3" x ¼")

Preschool children should have about one ounce of meat, poultry or seafood per day for each year of age.

Use poultry (without the skin) and fish more often than red meat.

Instead of high-fat luncheon meats, choose low-fat processed sandwich meats with *labels showing no more than 2 grams fat per ounce* such as turkey ▲ or chicken roll ▲, turkey ham ▲, turkey pastrami ▲ or lean boiled ham ▲

Buy only the leanest ground beef, *labeled as containing no more than 15% fat*. Pour off the fat after browning. Ask your butcher for the fat content, if it is not noted on the label.

Skim the fat off meat juices before adding to stews, soups and gravy. Chilling the meat juices first allows you to easily remove the hardened fat.

Foods to Avoid:

Meats—"Prime" grade and other heavily-marbled and fatty meats such as corned beef ■, regular pastrami ■, short ribs, spareribs, rib eye roast or steak, regular ground meat, frankfurters ■, sausage ■ bacon ■ and high-fat luncheon meats ■

Goose and Domestic Duck

Organ Meats—Brains, chitterlings, gizzard, heart, kidney, sweetbreads, pork maws and liver are high in cholesterol. However, liver is so rich in iron and vitamins, a small serving (3 ounces) is recommended about once a month.

Desserts, Beverages & Snacks

Okay Foods:

The foods listed here are low in saturated fat and cholesterol but many are high in calories and low in nutritional value. Use the foods from the other five food lists to make your eating plan. Then occasionally choose a few of the foods listed below to add interest. For weight control, select from the first two lists. If you are at your recommended weight, add selections from the "Other Choices" list.

First Choice (low in calories or no calories)—Raw vegetables, fresh fruit, fruit canned without sugar, plain gelatin, tea, coffee and cocoa powder.

Second Choice (low in saturated fat, fairly low in calories)—Frozen or canned fruit with sugar, dried fruits; seeds; "Okay" nuts ●; plain popcorn ●; pretzels ●; "Okay" crackers ● or cookies; sherbet, ice milk; frozen or fruited low-fat yogurt; angel food cake.

Other Choices (higher in calories)
Foods that are low in fat, also low in nutrition—Hard candy, gum drops; flavored gelatin; water ices; fruit punches, carbonated drinks; sugar, syrup, honey, jam, jelly, marmalade.

Special recipe items—Home-made desserts (cakes, pies, cookies and puddings) made with the fats and oils, low-fat milk products and egg products listed as "Okay."

Alcoholic beverages—If you drink, do so in moderation; no more than two drinks per day of wine, beer or liquor.

Foods To Avoid:

Other desserts and snacks not listed above, such as store-bought cakes, pies, cookies and mixes; coconut; high-fat snack products such as deep fried chips ■ and rich crackers ■; desserts and snacks containing cheese ■, cream or whole milk, and ice cream.

Be Salt-Wise

The following codes used in the food lists identify store-bought foods which are usually very high in salt or fat.

▲ means that although the food is okay for occasional use, it has a high salt content which cannot be removed.

● means the food usually contains salt, but good low-salt products are available.

■ means the food is high in *both* salt and dietary fat and cholesterol, making it a very poor food choice.

Reproduced with permission
© *The American Heart Association Diet*
American Heart Association

Food Tables

Food/Portion	Calories	Total Fat (grams)	Saturated Fat (grams)	Protein (grams)	Carbohydrates (grams)	Cholesterol (milligrams)
POULTRY, SEAFOOD & MEATS						
Chicken						
Breast, meat and skin, roasted (3½ oz.)	195	8	2.2	30	0	83
Breast, meat only, roasted (3½ oz.)	164	4	1.0	31	0	84
Thigh, meat and skin, roasted (3½ oz.)	245	15	4.3	25	0	92
Thigh, meat only, roasted (3½ oz.)	207	11	3.0	26	0	94
Liver, simmered (3½ oz.)	156	5	1.8	24	1	626
Turkey						
Light meat, meat and skin, roasted (3½ oz.)	188	7	2.1	28	0	73
Light meat, meat only, roasted (3½ oz.)	153	3	0.9	30	0	68
Dark meat, meat and skin, roasted (3½ oz.)	216	11	3.3	28	0	91
Dark meat, meat only, roasted (3½ oz.)	184	7	2.3	28	0	87
Giblets—gizzard, heart, liver, simmered (3½ oz.)	166	5	1.5	26	2	415
Ground, cooked (3½ oz.)	223	13	4.5	26	0	91
Ground, skinned breast meat only, cooked (3½ oz.)	153	3	0.9	30	0	68
Goose						
Meat and skin, roasted (3½ oz.)	303	22	6.8	25	0	90
Meat only, roasted (3½ oz.)	236	13	4.5	29	0	95
Duck						
Meat and skin, roasted (3½ oz.)	334	28	9.6	19	0	83
Meat only, roasted (3½ oz.)	199	11	4.1	23	0	88
Finfish						
Cod, Atlantic, cooked, dry heat (3½ oz.)	104	1	0.2	23	0	55
Flounder, cooked, dry heat (3½ oz.)	116	2	0.4	24	0	67
Halibut, cooked, dry heat (3½ oz.)	139	3	0.4	26	0	41
Mackerel, cooked, dry heat (3½ oz.)	260	18	4.2	24	0	74
Redfish, cooked, dry heat (3½ oz.)	120	2	0.3	24	0	54
Salmon, sockeye, grilled (3½ oz.)	216	11	1.9	27	0	87
Sea bass, cooked, dry heat (3½ oz.)	123	3	0.7	23	0	53
Snapper, cooked, dry heat (3½ oz.)	127	2	0.4	26	0	47
Swordfish, cooked, dry heat (3½ oz.)	154	5	1.4	25	0	50
Trout, rainbow, cooked, dry heat (3½ oz.)	150	4	0.8	26	0	72
Tuna, white, canned in oil, drained (3½ oz.)	185	8	N/A	26	0	31
Tuna, white, canned in water, drained (3½ oz.)	135	2	0.6	26	0	42

*Contains less than 1 gram.

Food/Portion	Calories	Total Fat (grams)	Saturated Fat (grams)	Protein (grams)	Carbohydrates (grams)	Cholesterol (milligrams)
Shellfish						
Clams, cooked, moist heat (3½ oz.)	147	2	0.2	25	5	66
Crab, Alaskan king, cooked, moist heat (3½ oz.)	96	2	0.1	19	0	53
Lobster, cooked, moist heat (3½ oz.)	97	1	0.1	20	1	71
Oysters, raw (3½ oz.)	68	2	0.6	7	4	55
Scallops, raw (3½ oz.)	87	1	0.1	17	2	33
Shrimp, cooked, moist heat (3½ oz.)	98	1	0.3	21	0	193
Beef						
Flank steak, lean only, broiled (3½ oz.)	241	15	6.3	25	0	69
Porterhouse, broiled (3½ oz.)	297	21	8.7	25	0	82
Prime rib, cooked (3½ oz.)	383	32	13.7	22	0	84
Round steak, lean only, broiled (3½ oz.)	193	8	2.9	28	0	81
Tenderloin, lean only, broiled (3½ oz.)	205	10	3.7	28	0	83
Ground, extra-lean, broiled (3½ oz.)	254	16	6.4	25	0	83
Ground, lean, broiled (3½ oz.)	270	18	7.2	25	0	86
Ground, regular, broiled (3½ oz.)	287	21	8.1	24	0	89
Liver, braised (3½ oz.)	160	5	1.9	24	3	386
Veal						
Ground, cooked (3½ oz.)	172	8	3.0	24	0	103
Loin chop, lean only, braised (3½ oz.)	226	9	2.6	34	0	125
Lamb						
Leg, shank portion, lean only, roasted (3½ oz.)	179	7	2.4	28	0	86
Loin chops, lean only, broiled (3½ oz.)	215	10	3.5	30	0	94
Rack rib, roasted (3½ oz.)	230	13	4.7	26	0	87
Pork						
Bacon, pan-fried (3½ oz.)	572	49	17.3	30	1	84
Canadian bacon, grilled (3½ oz.)	184	8	2.8	24	1	58
Fresh pork, lean only (3½ oz.)	219	11	3.6	29	0	95
Center loin, broiled (3½ oz.)	314	22	8.0	27	0	96
Shoulder, roasted (3½ oz.)	323	25	9.2	22	0	95
Tenderloin, roasted (3½ oz.)	165	5	1.7	29	0	92
Ham, boneless, canned, roasted (3½ oz.)	226	15	5.0	21	★	62
Spareribs, braised (3½ oz.)	394	30	11.7	29	0	120
LUNCHEON MEAT, SAUSAGE						
Bologna, beef (1 oz.)	89	8	3.3	3	1	16
Bologna, pork (1 oz.)	70	6	2.0	4	★	17
Frankfurter, beef (1 oz.)	89	8	3.4	3	1	17
Frankfurter, beef & pork (1 oz.)	91	8	3.1	3	1	14
Frankfurter, chicken (1 oz.)	73	6	1.6	4	2	29
Pepperoni (1 oz.)	141	12	4.6	6	1	22
Salami, dry (1 oz.)	119	10	3.5	6	1	22
Sausage, Italian, pork, cooked (1 oz.)	92	7	2.6	6	★	22
Sausage, liverwurst, pork (1 oz.)	92	8	3.0	4	1	45

*Contains less than 1 gram.

Food/Portion	Calories	Total Fat (grams)	Saturated Fat (grams)	Protein (grams)	Carbohydrates (grams)	Cholesterol (milligrams)
FRUIT						
Apple (1 med.)	81	★	0.1	★	21	0
Apricots, dried (8 halves)	67	★	0	1	17	0
Avocado (1 med.)	324	31	4.9	4	15	0
Banana (1 med.)	105	1	0.2	1	27	0
Cantaloupe (½ cup)	28	★	N/A	1	7	0
Cherries, sweet (10 large)	49	1	0.2	1	11	0
Dates, dried (2)	46	★	N/A	★	12	0
Figs, fresh (1 med.)	37	★	0	★	10	0
Grapefruit (½ grapefruit)	38	★	0	1	10	0
Grapes, tight skinned (15)	57	★	0.2	★	14	0
Orange, peeled (1 med.)	69	★	0.1	1	17	0
Peach (1 med.)	56	★	0	1	15	0
Pear, Bartlett (1 med.)	98	1	0	1	25	0
Pineapple, fresh (½ cup)	38	★	0	★	10	0
Plum (1 med.)	36	★	0	1	9	0
Prunes, dried (3)	60	★	0	★	16	0
Raisins (2 tbsp.)	54	★	0	★	14	0
Raspberries (½ cup)	30	★	0	★	7	0
Strawberries (½ cup)	23	★	0	★	5	0
Watermelon (½ cup)	26	★	N/A	1	6	0
VEGETABLES						
Artichokes, globe, cooked (1 med.)	53	★	0	3	12	0
Asparagus, fresh, cooked (½ cup)	23	★	0	2	4	0
Beans, green, fresh, cooked (½ cup)	22	★	0	1	5	0
Beans, lima, large dry, cooked (½ cup)	109	★	0.1	7	20	0
Broccoli, fresh, cooked (½ cup)	23	★	0	2	4	0
Cabbage, green, raw, shredded (½ cup)	8	★	0	★	2	0
Carrots, fresh, raw (½ cup)	24	★	0	1	6	0
Corn, fresh, cooked (½ cup)	89	1	0.2	3	21	0
Lettuce, green leaf (½ cup)	5	★	0	★	1	0
Mushrooms, fresh, raw (½ cup)	9	★	0	1	2	0
Peas, green, frozen, cooked (½ cup)	62	★	0	4	11	0
Pepper, bell, chopped (½ cup)	13	★	0	★	3	0
Potato, baked with skin (1 med.)	220	★	0.1	5	51	0
Potato, boiled, peeled (½ cup)	68	★	0	1	16	0
Potato, sweet, baked in skin, peeled (1 med.)	120	★	0	2	28	0
Spinach, fresh, raw (½ cup)	6	★	0	1	1	0
Squash, summer, fresh, cooked (½ cup)	18	★	0	1	4	0
Squash, winter, fresh, cooked (½ cup)	40	1	0.1	1	9	0
Tomatoes, fresh (½ cup)	17	★	0	1	4	0

*Contains less than 1 gram.

Food/Portion	Calories	Total Fat (grams)	Saturated Fat (grams)	Protein (grams)	Carbohydrates (grams)	Cholesterol (milligrams)
BREADS, PASTA, GRAINS, LEGUMES, NUTS						
Bread, rye (1 oz.)	69	*	0.3	3	15	*
Bread, white, enriched (1 oz.)	77	1	0.2	2	14	1
Bread, whole wheat (1 oz.)	69	1	0.2	3	14	1
Crackers, graham (4 squares)	109	3	0.6	2	21	0
Crackers, saltine (10)	123	3	0.8	3	20	0
Doughnut, raised, glazed (1)	170	10	2.4	2	19	11
English muffin (1)	130	1	N/A	4	26	0
Roll, frankfurter or hamburger (1)	119	2	0.5	3	21	2
Roll, hard (1)	156	2	0.4	5	30	2
Tortilla, corn (1)	67	1	N/A	2	13	0
Macaroni, cooked (½ cup)	78	*	N/A	2	16	0
Noodles, egg, cooked (½ cup)	100	1	N/A	3	19	25
Rice, brown, cooked (½ cup)	116	1	N/A	2	25	0
Rice, white, enriched, cooked (½ cup)	112	*	0	2	25	0
Beans, black, dried, cooked (½ cup)	114	*	0.1	8	20	0
Beans, pinto, dried, cooked (½ cup)	117	*	0.1	7	22	0
Lentils, dried, cooked (½ cup)	115	*	0.5	9	20	0
Soybeans, dried, cooked (½ cup)	149	8	1.1	14	9	0
Almonds, whole, shelled (1 oz.)	167	15	1.4	6	6	0
Cashews, salted, roasted in oil (1 oz.)	163	14	2.7	5	8	0
Peanuts, salted, roasted in oil (1 oz.)	165	14	1.9	7	5	0
Peanut butter (1 tbsp.)	95	8	1.4	5	3	0
Pecans, halves (1 oz.)	189	19	1.5	2	5	0
Walnuts, English, pieces (1 oz.)	182	18	1.6	4	5	0

Food/Portion	Calories	Total Fat (grams)	Saturated Fat (grams)	Monounsaturated Fat (grams)	Polyunsaturated Fat (grams)	Cholesterol (milligrams)
OILS						
Canola (rapeseed) (1 tbsp.)	120	14	0.7–0.9	7.6–9.3	3.1–4.5	0
Coconut (1 tbsp.)	120	14	11.8	0.8	0.2	0
Corn (1 tbsp.)	120	14	1.7	3.3	8.0	0
Cottonseed (1 tbsp.)	120	14	3.5	2.4	7.1	0
Grapeseed (1 tbsp.)	120	14	1.3	2.2	9.5	0
Olive (1 tbsp.)	120	14	1.8	10.0	1.1	0
Palm (1 tbsp.)	120	14	6.7	5.0	1.3	0
Palm kernel (1 tbsp.)	120	14	11.1	1.5	0.2	0
Peanut (1 tbsp.)	120	14	2.3	6.2	4.3	0
Safflower (1 tbsp.)	120	14	1.2	1.7	10.2	0
Sesame (1 tbsp.)	120	14	1.9	5.4	5.7	0
Soybean (1 tbsp.)	120	14	2.0	5.9	5.1	0
Sunflower (1 tbsp.)	120	14	1.4	6.2	5.5	0
Walnut (1 tbsp.)	120	14	1.3	3.1	8.7	0

*Contains less than 1 gram.

Food/Portion	Calories	Total Fat (grams)	Saturated Fat (grams)	Protein (grams)	Carbohydrates (grams)	Cholesterol (milligrams)
OTHER FATS, EGGS, DAIRY						
Butter (1 tbsp.)	102	12	7.2	★	0	31
Lard (1 tbsp.)	116	13	5.0	0	0	12
Margarine, corn oil, hard (stick) (1 tbsp.)	102	11	1.9	★	0	0
Margarine, safflower oil, soft (tub) (1 tbsp.)	101	11	1.2	0	0	0
Mayonnaise, whole-egg (1 tbsp.)	99	11	1.6	★	★	8
Vegetable shortening, hydrogenated (1 tbsp.)	113	13	3.2	0	0	0
Egg, whole, raw (1 large)	75	5	1.6	6	.6	213
Egg yolk, raw (1)	59	5	1.6	3	★	213
Egg white, raw (1)	16	★	0	3	★	0
Buttermilk, cultured (1 cup)	98	2	1.4	8	12	10
Condensed milk, sweetened, canned (¼ cup)	246	7	4.2	6	42	26
Evaporated milk, skim, canned (¼ cup)	50	★	0.1	5	7	3
Evaporated milk, whole, canned (¼ cup)	84	5	2.9	4	6	18
Milk, whole (1 cup)	149	8	5.1	8	11	34
Milk, lowfat, 2% fat (1 cup)	122	5	2.9	8	12	20
Milk, skim or nonfat (1 cup)	86	★	0.3	8	12	5
Milk, whole, chocolate (1 cup)	208	8	5.3	8	26	30
Creamer, nondairy, liquid (1 tbsp.)	20	2	0.3	★	2	0
Creamer, nondairy, powder (1 tbsp.)	32	2	1.9	★	3	0
Half & half (1 tbsp.)	20	2	1.1	★	1	6
Sour cream (1 tbsp.)	31	3	1.9	★	3	6
Sour cream, light (1 tbsp.)	18	1	N/A	1	1	4
Whipping cream (1 tbsp.)	51	6	3.4	★	★	20
Whipped cream, pressurized (1 tbsp.)	10	1	0.5	★	★	3
Dessert topping, nondairy (1 tbsp.)	9	1	0.5	★	1	1
Yogurt, whole, plain (8 oz.)	138	7	4.8	8	11	29
Yogurt, lowfat, plain (8 oz.)	143	4	2.3	12	16	14
Yogurt, lowfat, fruit-flavored (8 oz.)	231	2	1.6	10	43	9
Yogurt, nonfat, plain (8 oz.)	127	★	0.3	13	17	5
Cheese						
American (1 oz.)	106	9	5.6	6	★	27
Blue (1 oz.)	100	8	5.3	6	1	21
Brie (1 oz.)	95	8	N/A	6	★	28
Cheddar (1 oz.)	114	9	6.0	7	★	30
Cheese spread, process, American (1 oz.)	82	6	3.8	5	2	16
Cottage cheese, creamed (½ cup)	108	5	3.0	13	3	16
Cottage cheese, dry curd (½ cup)	62	★	0.2	13	1	5
Cottage cheese, lowfat, 2% fat (½ cup)	102	2	1.4	16	4	9
Cream cheese (1 oz.)	99	10	6.2	2	1	31
Gouda (1 oz.)	101	8	5.0	7	1	32
Gruyère (1 oz.)	117	9	5.4	8	★	31
Jack (1 oz.)	106	9	N/A	7	★	25
Mozzarella, whole milk (1 oz.)	80	6	3.7	6	★	22
Mozzarella, part skim (1 oz.)	72	5	2.9	7	1	16
Neufchâtel (1 oz.)	74	7	4.2	3	1	22
Parmesan (1 oz.)	129	9	5.4	12	1	22

*Contains less than 1 gram.

Food/Portion	Calories	Total Fat (grams)	Saturated Fat (grams)	Protein (grams)	Carbohydrates (grams)	Cholesterol (milligrams)
Cheese (continued)						
Ricotta, whole milk (½ cup)	214	16	10.2	14	4	63
Ricotta, part skim (½ cup)	170	10	6.1	14	6	38
Roquefort (1 oz.)	105	9	5.5	6	1	26
Swiss (1 oz.)	107	8	5.0	8	1	26
Frozen Desserts						
Frozen yogurt, lowfat (½ cup)	100	3	N/A	2	17	3
Frozen yogurt, nonfat (½ cup)	80	0	0	3	18	0
Ice cream, rich, 16% fat (½ cup)	175	12	7.4	2	16	44
Ice cream, regular, 10% fat (½ cup)	134	7	4.5	2	16	30
Ice milk, regular (½ cup)	92	3	1.8	3	14	9
Ice milk, soft serve (½ cup)	112	2	1.4	4	19	7
Sherbet, orange (½ cup)	135	2	1.2	1	29	7
Candy						
Caramels (1 oz.)	113	3	1.6	1	22	1
Chocolate, milk, plain (1 oz.)	147	9	5.1	2	16	6
Gumdrops (1 oz.)	98	*	N/A	0	25	0
Hard candy (1 oz.)	109	*	N/A	0	28	0

*Contains less than 1 gram.

Herbs & Spices

Allspice. Compatible foods: Ham, sweet potatoes, winter squash, sweet pickles, relishes, cakes, cookies.

Basil. Compatible foods: Poultry, omelets, tomato-based soups, sauces, and pasta dishes, artichokes, eggplant, spinach, fresh tomatoes, zucchini, salad dressings.

Bay leaves. Compatible foods: Meat loaf, stews, soups.

Cinnamon. Compatible foods: Sweet potatoes, winter squash, fruit compote, custards, cakes, pies, cookies.

Cloves. Compatible foods: Ham, barbecue sauce, spaghetti sauce, sweet pickles, relishes, cakes, cookies.

Cumin. Compatible foods: Curries; Mexican, Middle Eastern, and Indian dishes.

Dill. Compatible foods: Salmon, shrimp, omelets, beets, cabbage, potatoes, cucumbers, vegetable salads, dips.

Marjoram. Compatible foods: Beef, veal, poultry, omelets, soufflés, vegetable soup, tomato-based soups and sauces, eggplant, summer squash, salad dressings.

Mint. Compatible foods: Lamb, veal, fruit salads, carrots, peas, spinach, candies, jellies, iced beverages.

Nutmeg. Compatible foods: Ground beef, soufflés, cream-based pasta dishes, white sauce, spinach, custard, cakes, cookies.

Oregano. Compatible foods: Grilled meats, stews, poultry stuffing, vegetable soups, bell peppers, tomato-based soups, sauces, and pasta dishes, salad dressings.

Parsley. Compatible foods: All meats, fish, poultry; soups, stews, omelets, scrambled eggs, pasta dishes, fresh vegetables, salads (cabbage, pasta, potato), salad dressings.

Rosemary. Compatible foods: Chicken, lamb, meat marinades, vegetable soups, broccoli, peas, potatoes.

Sage. Compatible foods: Veal, sausage, poultry, mild white fish, pork, game, poultry stuffings, lima beans, mushrooms, onions.

Tarragon. Compatible foods: Veal, lamb, chicken, mild white fish, crab, shrimp, eggs, soufflés, soups, asparagus, mushrooms, béarnaise sauce, salad dressings.

Thyme. Compatible foods: Beef, pork, poultry, mild white fish, vegetable soups, tomato-based soups and sauces, carrots, green beans, mushrooms, salad dressings.

Substitutions to Reduce Fat & Cholesterol

Original	Substitute
Beef, regular ground	Extra-lean ground beef or ground skinned turkey breast
Butter	Polyunsaturated margarine with liquid oil listed as the first ingredient
Buttermilk	For every cup, use 1 tablespoon lemon juice or vinegar plus enough nonfat milk to equal 1 cup; or use lowfat buttermilk
Cheese	Lowfat cheeses, such as part-skim mozzarella and part-skim ricotta; use Parmesan in small quantities
Chicken, whole	Skinned chicken breast
Chocolate, unsweetened	For each ounce, use 3 tablespoons unsweetened cocoa plus 1 tablespoon salad oil
Cream	Evaporated skim milk
Cream, whipped (for topping)	Whipped Topping (page 76)
Egg, whole	For each whole egg, use 2 egg whites
French fries	Oven-baked Hash Browns (page 85)
Ice cream	Frozen lowfat yogurt, fruit ices, and sherbets
Milk, whole	Nonfat milk
Peanuts	Pretzels
Potato chips	Air-popped corn, plain
Salad dressings	Lowfat commercial dressings or homemade dressings, such as Spicy French Dressing (page 76)
Shortening, solid vegetable	Vegetable oil
Sour cream	Nonfat plain yogurt or lowfat sour cream
Tuna packed in oil	Tuna packed in water

How to Read Food Labels

No cholesterol! No fat! These claims are made for many foods. How do you verify and interpret these statements? When you're purchasing any canned or packaged good, it pays to be able to understand and interpret nutrition labels, especially when it comes to calculating the percentage of calories that come from fat.

Nutrition information must be provided for any food for which health claims are made, or to which nutrients have been added. The information is given in a standard form. The serving size and servings per container are listed, followed by the calorie, protein, carbohydrate, and fat content per serving; amounts of sodium, cholesterol, and saturated and unsaturated fat may or may not be presented. Next, the label shows the percentage of the U.S. Recommended Daily Allowances for protein, vitamins, and minerals provided by one serving. Finally, the ingredients are listed in descending order by weight.

Determining the calorie breakdown.
Look at the following hypothetical label information, similar to what you might find on a snack food package.

Nutrition Information Per Serving:

Serving size: 1 oz.
Servings per container: 4
Calories: 160
Protein (grams): 3
Carbohydrates (grams): 12
Fat (grams): 11
Sodium (milligrams): 10
Cholesterol (milligrams): 0

To calculate the percentage of calories from fat in any food, multiply the number of grams of fat per serving by 9—in our example, 11 x 9 = 99. Divide the fat calories by the total calories: 99 ÷ 160 = .62. Then multiply this figure by 100 to find the percent: .62 x 100 = 62%. Keep in mind that the American Heart Association (AHA) recommends that no more than 30% of your daily calories come from fat.

The AHA also recommends that about 55% of the day's calories come from carbohydrates. To determine carbohydrate calories, multiply the grams of carbohydrate per serving by 4—in our case, 12 x 4 = 48. Then follow the procedure just outlined for fat: divide your answer by the total calories and multiply by 100 to get the percentage. Thus, 48 ÷ 160 = .30; .30 x 100 = 30%. You can use the same method to determine the percent of protein calories, since protein, like carbohydrates, provides about 4 calories per gram.

What you've learned from our sample label, then, is that the product, though cholesterol-free, contains about 62% fat and 30% carbohydrates—just about the reverse of the situation you'd like to see for daily calorie intake. Because cutting down on fat is important in reducing cholesterol, you'd be better off looking for a product that is not only low in cholesterol but also lower in fat—and higher in carbohydrates.

Using the ingredient list.
You can read the ingredient list to confirm claims stated about a food. For instance, if no ingredients from animal sources are listed, the food can be accurately described as cholesterol-free. However, it may still be high in saturated fats, which tend to raise blood cholesterol levels.

You can also use the list in other ways. To limit your intake of saturated fat, for example, choose a margarine that lists partially hydrogenated oil *after* liquid oil; that way you'll be getting more unsaturated fat than saturated (remember that the label lists ingredients in descending order by weight).

Be aware that manufacturers are permitted to list fats with the explanation "contains one or more of the following." If you're trying to avoid saturated fat, you may decide not to purchase a product that lists in its ingredients a statement such as "contains one or more of the following: soybean and/or palm kernel oil." Such a statement doesn't tell you whether saturated, unsaturated, or both fats are used in the food.

Take care of your heart by using your head—read labels carefully.

How Many Calories Per Day?

To determine what your daily caloric intake should be, you'll need to know your frame size—small, medium, or large. Extend your arm and bend the forearm up at a 90° angle. Keeping the fingers straight, turn the inside of your wrist toward your body. Place the thumb and index finger of your other hand on the two prominent bones on either side of your elbow. Measure the space between your fingers against a ruler or a tape measure. Compare this figure with the measurements for a medium frame, shown below. Measurements lower than those listed mean you have a small frame; higher measurements indicate a large frame. Once you've determined your frame size, use the second chart to find your desirable weight.

Frame Size

Men

Height (without shoes)	Elbow Breadth
5'1"–5'2"	2½"–2⅞"
5'3"–5'6"	2⅝"–2⅞"
5'7"–5'10"	2¾"–3"
5'11"–6'2"	2¾"–3⅛"
6'3"	2⅞"–3¼"

Women

Height (without shoes)	Elbow Breadth
4'9"–4'10"	2¼"–2½"
4'11"–5'2"	2¼"–2½"
5'3"–5'6"	2⅜"–2⅝"
5'7"–5'10"	2⅜"–2⅝"

Desirable Body Weight Ranges

Men

Height (without shoes)	Weight (without clothes) Small Frame (pounds)	Medium Frame (pounds)	Large Frame (pounds)
5'1"	105–113	111–122	119–134
5'2"	108–116	114–126	122–137
5'3"	111–119	117–129	125–141
5'4"	114–122	120–132	128–145
5'6"	121–130	127–140	135–154
5'7"	125–134	131–145	140–159
5'8"	129–138	135–149	144–163
5'9"	133–143	139–153	148–167
5'10"	137–147	143–158	152–172
5'11"	141–151	147–163	157–177
6'0"	145–155	151–168	161–182
6'1"	149–160	155–173	166–187
6'2"	153–164	160–178	171–192
6'3"	157–168	165–183	175–197

Women

Height (without shoes)	Weight (without clothes) Small Frame (pounds)	Medium Frame (pounds)	Large Frame (pounds)
4'9"	90–97	94–106	102–118
4'10"	92–100	97–109	105–121
4'11"	95–103	100–112	108–124
5'0"	98–106	103–115	111–127
5'1"	101–109	106–118	114–130
5'2"	104–112	109–122	117–134
5'3"	107–115	112–126	121–138
5'4"	110–119	116–131	125–142
5'5"	114–123	120–135	129–146
5'6"	118–127	124–139	133–150
5'7"	122–131	128–143	137–154
5'8"	126–136	132–147	141–159
5'9"	130–140	136–151	145–164
5'10"	134–144	140–155	149–169

Source: 1959 Metropolitan Desirable Weight Table, courtesy of Metropolitan Life Insurance Company

To determine how many calories you should eat daily, multiply your desirable weight by 14 if you are a man, by 12 if you are a woman. For example, a 5'10" man with a small frame should weigh 137 to 147 pounds; thus, he should consume 1,918 to 2,058 calories per day. A 5'10" woman with a small frame should weigh 134 to 144 pounds and eat 1,608 to 1,728 calories per day.

If you find that you're not in your correct weight range, you may want to consider losing weight. Start by consulting your physician for any specific advice. In general, you can determine the number of calories per day appropriate for a weight loss regimen by multiplying your desirable weight by 10; for example, if you should weigh 125 pounds, your diet should provide 1,250 calories daily.

You can cut your caloric intake by substituting foods high in complex carbohydrates for those high in fat, since fat has more than twice as many calories per gram as do carbohydrates or protein. Beyond decreasing the total calories in your daily diet, adopt a regular exercise program for successful long-term weight loss and maintenance.

Index